D1345793

OEDIPUS AT COLONUS

Uniform with this volume

SOPHOCLES
Oedipus, King of Thebes
24th Thousand
The Antigone
4th Thousand
The Wife of Heracles
3rd Thousand

EURIPIDES
Alcestis
24th Thousand
Bacchae
31st Thousand
Electra
50th Thousand
Hippolytus
38th Thousand
Iphigenia in Tauris
32nd Thousand
Medea
33rd Thousand
Rhesus
9th Thousand
The Trojan Women
39th Thousand

ARISTOPHANES
The Frogs
24th Thousand

AESCHYLUS
Agamemnon
12th Thousand
The Choëphoroe
5th Thousand
The Eumenides
4th Thousand
The Suppliant Women (Supplices)
4th Thousand
Prometheus Bound
4th Thousand
The Seven Against Thebes
3rd Thousand
The Persians
4th Thousand

★

The Oresteia
Collected Edition

SOPHOCLES

OEDIPUS AT COLONUS

Translated into English rhyming verse

with Introduction and Notes

by

GILBERT MURRAY

O.M., D.C.L.

*Formerly Regius Professor of Greek
in the
University of Oxford*

London

GEORGE ALLEN & UNWIN LTD

PRINTED IN GREAT BRITAIN
in 11-Point Caslon Old Face
BY UNWIN BROTHERS LIMITED
WOKING

PREFACE

THE *Oedipus at Colonus** has often been compared with
King Lear. It is not only that both plays have for their
central figure an old, dethroned and banished king,
driven mad or half-mad by his awful experiences, and
breathing a strange atmosphere of kingly pride alterna-
ting with helplessness, of towering passion with profound
peace. In both also the suffering hero achieves a sort
of change or conversion. "The poem," says Professor
Dowden, "might well be named the redemption of
Lear" and in a sense the present play shows the
redemption of Oedipus. But whereas Lear repents of
his pride and self-will and is brought "to kinship and
sympathy with all afflicted humanity," Oedipus feels
no need to repent for his involuntary acts of pollution,
but by unflinching endurance of the evils laid upon him
by mysterious gods, he is transformed from an outcast
to a hero, from a despised and unclean wanderer to an
object of adoration and dread. It is significant that
both plays make heavy, if not impossible, demands on
the producer for tempests and thunderstorms. And of
both it may be said, that, while neither can quite be
called a "well-made play," each nevertheless contains
some of the author's very greatest work.

Greek tradition tells us that the play was produced
by the poet's grandson, Sophocles the younger, four

---

* The two plays are generally known by their Latin names, *Oedipus
Rex*, (Oedipus, king) and *Oedipus Coloneüs*, (Oedipus of Colônus).

5

years after the author's death at the age of ninety. This is confirmed by the metrical and linguistic tests, which clearly prove the *Colonêüs* to be among the last of the poet's writings; indeed it would almost seem that some parts of the play required a fourth actor, unless we escape that startling conclusion by the somewhat evasive hypothesis of a supernumerary *persona muta* who was not always entirely mute.* The play certainly leaves the impression of coming from one who has largely left the turmoil of life behind him and looks back upon it with deepened understanding and mature mastery of language and poetry.

Some modern readers have seen signs of old age in a certain lengthiness and lack of concentration in the drama. It is, as Aristotle would say, "episodic," and each episode involves some dissipation of interest. The ancient critics, however, seem to have singled out the "oeconomia"—the construction or management—of the play for particular admiration. Aristophanes of Byzantium considered that in this respect it had no equal. He might have pointed out that it contains many characters, none of them mere vessels of rhetoric but each with his own *ethos* and his own purposes and a good reason for entering when he does. And it is true that each episode serves its purpose in showing the gradual sanctification or "heroization" of Oedipus. A hero was by no means necessarily a lovable character; he had to be firstly, uncanny and different from common men, and secondly formidable, with powers to injure

* Called by Pollux (4, 110) a *"parachorêgêma"* or "extra supplement."

or to bless, connected always with a taboo grave. So far he is like a mediaeval saint; but he need not be saintly in character. Aegisthus and Salmoneus, famous for their sins, were "heroes." An extreme case is that of the athlete Cleomêdês, who, after killing his opponent, went mad and destroyed a school with sixty children in it; naturally people were afraid of such a being and felt it desirable to "appease" his tomb. The terrific cursing of Polynices by his father, which was heartbreaking to Antigone, seems to us a very strange prelude to the scene of something like sanctification which immediately follows, but of course heroization is not the same thing as sanctification. The curse showed how truly formidable the inmate of that mysterious tomb was to be; and we must always remember that in an insecure and unpoliced society, like those of antiquity in general, the punishment of the wicked was a keenly felt social necessity. Was the wrong-doer to go scot-free, and the cry of the "wronged ones in the darkness" to be left unheard? A true hero must curse as well as bless.

Though not in any sense part of a trilogy, the *Coloneüs* has an obvious connection with two other Sophoclean plays. The *Oedipus Rex*, produced some twenty years earlier, had ended on a raw and painful note. The blinded man's last words, when all else has been taken from him, are a cry, "Ah no; take not away my daughters"; and they are immediately taken. This harsh "curtain" is against the normal practice of Greek Art, which likes to end on a note of calm, and it may well be that Sophocles in his old age wished, as a sort of atonement, to let the agonized and accursed hero of his greatest drama attain, as it were, a special position of reconciliation with God. The *Antigone* also, which was even earlier than the first Oedipus, was clearly in the mind of the poet when writing this play. The Polynices scenes, and especially the final speeches of the two sisters, are clearly meant to lead up to the situation in the beginning of the *Antigone*. Indeed the unusual obviousness of this technique in the last scene has led some scholars to suspect its genuineness. It is a curious coincidence that the final scene of Aeschylus' *Seven against Thebes* also seems to have been altered so as to suit the *Antigone*.

In many Greek tragedies a modern reader is struck by what is loosely called the "modernity" of the general tone. It is really the permanent human feeling which rises above the temporary conventions of a particular age. In such cases the dramatic sympathy, the conception of what is good or evil, in the ancient author falls naturally into sympathy with that of an enlightened European of the present day. In the *Prometheus* of Aeschylus, the *Trojan Women* or the *Hippolytus* of Euripides, the theme is one that still disturbs us, and the poet's attitude towards it is what we naturally expect. With Sophocles we have much more often to make the effort of putting ourselves imaginatively in an ancient, or what used to be called a "pagan," position. He seems to be untouched by the sophistic movement, untouched by Socrates, of course quite untouched by Plato. He seems to be full of a correct or even a primitive piety. He makes no attempt to moralize his gods or to pass any moral judgement upon them. They are mostly terrifying, and often inexplicably malignant. Of course we must remember that he is an artist, not a philosopher. He does, far more than the other two tragedians, make a practice of deepening the darkness of his tragic situations both by an insistence on physical pain or horror and by making full use of the mysterious terrors of that irrational primitive religion to which Oedipus's parricide and incest were not offences or errors capable of being rationally thought about but monstrous and inhuman pollutions, the last limit of imaginable sin. The cultivated Athenian of Sophocles' time had largely, though not entirely, escaped from these primitive ways of thought; the philosophic movements of the last two generations had done their work of enlightenment. Theseus is above such things here, as he is in Euripides' *Heracles*. He is not only, as always, a good democrat as well as a King, but also a King of the heroic age who has nevertheless had the advantage of an education in fifth-century philosophy. It is worth noticing, however, that to the Chorus Oedipus has repeatedly to labour the point of his lack of intention or knowledge and consequent lack of guilt (ll. 266 ff., 540 ff., 960–1000). Even so he is only partially successful. Though excused, and even accepted as a citizen of Athens, he is still no normal man. Innocent or not, the atmosphere of his awful doings stays about him. The play is full of the in-

9

fectiousness of the untouchable, whether it be too polluted and evil to leave anyone in its close neighbourhood safe, or too holy to be approached with impunity, like the shrine of the Eumenides. In the Book of Samuel, we may remember, Uzzah was struck dead when, with the best intentions, he touched the Ark of God. (II Sam. vi. 7). The conceptions, which seem to us utterly different, are equally combined in such words as the Roman *sacer*, or the Polynesian *taboo*. Oedipus is *araios*, charged with a curse or *Ara* as a wire may be charged with electricity, not only because he is himself accursed, but also because he is an old, blind, helpless, and deeply-wronged man, and thus has much of the sacredness of a suppliant. To touch or even look upon (l. 1480–1484) one so unholy may be fatal; to do wrong to one so afflicted is an abominable offence. His curse, unlike those of Lear upon his children, acts like a law. Those upon Creon (l. 870, "an old age such as mine") and Polynices were both completely fulfilled.

Connected with this power of the curse is the power of the *taboo* grave. The grave of a specially holy or unholy man is itself *araios*, charged with a curse. The bones of saints are still a valuable possession in some eastern countries, both Christian and Moslem. Indeed there have been cases where a saint has been, if not murdered, at least encouraged to die *in situ* by his admirers, in order to get possession of his remains. The graves of Eurystheus in the *Heraclidae*, of Orestes in the *Eumenides*, and of Oedipus here, are all to be a great defence to Athens, because any foreign invader, not knowing their position nor the correct ritual for appeasing them, would pretty certainly violate them and thus incur the wrath of the dead. The rightful possessor would give them the proper tendance and thus secure protection. The Thebans tried to play a double game; to exclude Oedipus from his native soil and yet to keep control over his grave. Theseus by his frank and merciful acceptance of the polluted suppliant seems, as it were, to nullify his pollution. One may compare his similar annulment of the pollution of his friend at the end of Euripides' *Heracles,* and a striking passage in the other *Oedipus* (ll. 1480 ff.) where no one dares to approach or even look upon the polluted and bloodstained man until the two little girls, not conscious of such things, throw themselves into his arms without fear. By that they have diverted the lightning and others can touch him too. Sophocles can use the philosophic ideas when it suits him, though he never obtrudes them.

Of the other characters, Antigone is the same loving and heroic girl as in the play that bears her name. If she is sometimes fierce she is fierce through love. There she faced death rather than fail her dead brother. Here she is ready for any ordeal rather than fail her blind father. It is worth noting that here too, she is a fighter. She stands up to the Colonean elders when her father has lost heart (l. 237), and stands up to him himself, unsparingly, when he refuses to see Polynices. The last scene of this play may throw light on a question which has often been raised in the *Antigone*. Is Antigone the older and stronger of the two sisters, Ismene the younger and weaker? Or, on the contrary, is Antigone the young passionate and impulsive girl, Ismene the elder and more prudent? Most scholars have taken the first view; but the scene between the sisters after l. 1669 strongly suggests the second.

Creon is not brought into any particular relation to the falsely accused Creon of the *Oedipus Rex* nor yet to the rigid conscientious tyrant of the *Antigone*. He belongs to a type peculiarly detested by the dramatists, both tragic and comic, of the later years of the Peloponnesian War, the hard-faced politician. We know that he is a ruthless hypocritical schemer, but he contrives almost always to have the *beau rôle* and to put his opponents in the wrong. His entrance is masterly. It is almost impossible to resist so reasonable a plea, so modestly urged. When he shows his teeth he gets the best of the repartees. When denounced by Theseus he maintains his dignity and his power of sarcasm; an old man, alone in a strange country he yields calmly to superior strength but reserves his full answer till he is on his own soil. The name "Creon" means merely "ruler," and that is what the Creon of legend always is; an official rather than a person; but the poets can give that colourless figure such character as it pleases them.

Polyniĉês is a character mainly created by his situation, the wronged warrior prince, determined at all costs to get his rights and indifferent to all else, ready to die if he must but incapable of making any concession; perhaps too weak to change, perhaps too heroic; mostly blind to things outside himself, though capable of penitence for his neglect of his father and of tender love for his two sisters.

The aged poet is said to have lived at Colonus, and this play is full of a special love for the actual neighbourhood of his home and the little religious rites and local sanctities that were centred there. No other play that has come down to us shows this sort of feeling, though we may be reminded of Horace's feeling for his Sabine farm. The sanctuary of the Eumenides, the grove where there is nearly always a nightingale, the two paths to the Theban border, the "brazen threshold" and the place midway between "the three-crested rock, the hollow pear-tree and the marble tomb," have by now become legendary; to Sophocles they were part of his home (l. 162);

> The fame thereof
> Was slender, but to know them was to love.

In an ancient Greek this love of the actual land and groves expressed itself naturally in local rituals of worship. The lists of deities and rites which Sophocles delights in often seem conventional and formal to us. Yet perhaps they are merely the natural expression of that "pagan" state of mind which was always ready to "have sight of Proteus rising from the sea" and from the sight to create both a ritual and a legend. The same love of the land merges easily into a national patriotism of the more ordinary sort. By the year in which the *Coloneüs* was written the Beloved City was in dire distress, and it was difficult for any Athenian not to feel her an almost sacred being beset by lawless and brutal foes. There is great artistic skill in the lyrics in which Sophocles celebrates these homely places and worships, but many will feel that his full genius emerges most in those which deal with the impersonal and eternal subjects, old age and death. The particular part which the various choral lyrics play in the development of the drama will be treated in the notes.

CHARACTERS IN THE PLAY

OEDIPUS, formerly King of Thebes, now exiled; son of Laïus and Jocasta.

ANTIGONÊ, his daughter.

ISMÊNÊ, his daughter.

POLYNÎCÊS, his eldest son.

CREON, brother of Jocasta; the chief influence in Thebes.

THÊSEUS, King of Athens, son of Aigeus.

AN ATHENIAN STRANGER.

A MESSENGER.

CHORUS of Elders of Colônus, with their LEADER.

"The Oedipus at Colonus *was produced after the death of the poet by his grandson, Sophocles, son of Ariston, in the archonship of Mikon* (402 B.C.), *who was fourth from Callias, in whose year of office most authorities say Sophocles died.*" THE ANCIENT ARGUMENT

SCENE

The Hill of COLONUS outside Athens. Back at the left the Grove of the Eumenides, a tangle of olive, laurel, and vine: further back at the right a view of the Acropolis. In front of the Grove, near the middle, a Rock in which a seat has been cut.

Enter *from spectators' left OEDIPUS, now an old man, with beggar's dress and wallet and staff, his hair long and wild, his eye-sockets empty. He is led by his daughter ANTIGONE, a girl about eighteen, poorly clad.*
The time is toward the close of day.

OEDIPUS

Child of an age-worn father and a blind,
What lands be these, what town of human kind?
What new folk now shall greet with hazardous
And stinted alms the outcast Oedipus,
Who craves but little of them, and yet less
Receiving is content? Longsufferingness
I have learnt by much pain, and the company
Of the slow years, and mine own royalty.
My child, if thou canst see some resting place,
Be it on ground profane or by the grace
Of God o'ershadowed, lead and set me there.
When some man passeth I will ask him where

17   B

We are come. We needs must hearken all they say
Whose lands we traverse, and their words obey.

ANTIGONE   [*Looking off.*

Father and king toil-worn, grey towers there are
Crowning a city—to mine eyes still far.
But where we stand the place is holy, green
With bay, olive and vine: and deep within
Are darting wings, and somewhere through the trees
A nightingale, all song. Come take thine ease
On this rough seat of stone. 'Tis a long way
For one so old, thy feet have fared to-day.

OEDIPUS

Aye, help me sit, and guard my darkness. So.   [*Sits.*

ANTIGONE

If time can teach, that lesson I should know.

OEDIPUS

Know'st thou at all the region where we are?

ANTIGONE

This spot, no. . . . It is Athens there afar.

OEDIPUS

So much we learned from every wayfarer.

ANTIGONE

Well, shall I leave thee and go ask somewhere?

OEDIPUS

Yes; ask, if 'tis a place where men may dwell.

ANTIGONE

Oh, 'tis inhabited.—Yet it were well
To wait. I see a man there within call.

OEDIPUS

Doth he come towards us? . . . Doth he move at all?

ANTIGONE

He soon will come . . . Now speak in question clear
What thy heart prompteth, for the man is here.

[*Enter* STRANGER.

OEDIPUS

Sir Stranger, hearing from this maid, whose eyes
Are hers and mine, that here in timely wise
Thou comest for the solving of our doubt . . .

STRANGER

Stay! Ere thou question further, get thee out
From here; 'tis holy ground, where none may sit.

OEDIPUS

What is the grove? And what God haunteth it?

STRANGER

Untouched it is, untrod. Dread Virgins hold
Their court here, born of Earth and Darkness old.

OEDIPUS

Who? Let me hear their names and I will pray.

STRANGER

    [Hesitating to pronounce the real name.
The all-seeing Spirits of Mercy, our folk say
In Athens: elsewhere other names they bear.

OEDIPUS   *[Suddenly kneeling.*

With mercy, then, may they accept and spare
Him who now kneels to them. Here I have found
My peace, and leave no more this holy ground.

STRANGER

What means this?

OEDIPUS

    'Tis the watchword of my fate.

STRANGER

For me, I dare not move thee till the state
Give warrant. They who rule must know thy deed.
    [He moves to go off.

OEDIPUS   [*Detaining him.*

Nay, keep not from an outcast in his need,
Stranger, the little knowledge that he sues.

STRANGER

Well; make thy questions. I shall not refuse.

OEDIPUS

Tell me, what is this region that we tread?

STRANGER

All that I know of it can soon be said.
All here is holy ground: men say our Sire
Poseidon treads it, and the Wand of Fire,
Titan Promêtheus, with him. Thou dost feel
The rock? The threshold of the Bronzen Heel
'Tis called, which guardeth Athens. On each hand
Men say the primal master of the land
Was old Colônus, he who first made tame
The war-horse. All the folk yet bear his name.
Such, stranger, are these hills. The fame thereof
Is slender, yet to know them is to love.

OEDIPUS

There be, then, folk who dwell and habit here?

STRANGER

Surely; Colônês is the name they bear.

21

OEDIPUS

Have they some lord, or doth the mass bear sway?

STRANGER

In Athens is the king these lands obey.

OEDIPUS

And what king there doth such obedience claim?

STRANGER

Old Aigeus' son, Theseus they call his name.

OEDIPUS

Will one of you bear him a word from me?

STRANGER

What word? Or wouldst thou bid him come to thee?

OEDIPUS

That little toil shall bring him great reward.

STRANGER

How can a man who sees not help our lord?

OEDIPUS

The words that I shall speak, they shall have eyes!

STRANGER

Stranger, I would not have thee anywise
Ill done by; for I see thou art a man
Noble, in all save fortune. For a span
Of time wait here; I will go forth and tell—
Not all the city, but the folk who dwell
Hard by, thy story. As their laws decide
Thou shalt depart this precinct, or abide.   [*Exit.*

OEDIPUS

Child, has the stranger left us?

ANTIGONE

                              Yes: speak on
In peace all thy desire. I am here alone.

OEDIPUS

                    [*Kneeling towards the Grove.*
O awful Eyes, O Shapes of Majesty,
To you before all else this bended knee
Its homage brings; be gracious for my sake
And Lord Apollo's too; who when he spake
Long since my doom of evil, made me blest
Still by the far-off promise of this rest;
In a last land, where They whom the world fears
Should spread a chair for me and make me theirs,
There this sore heart should rest and have an end;
To them that shelter me a powerful friend,

23

To them that drave me outcast from my home
A curse undying. And a sign shall come,
So vowed he, or strange thunder, or the ground
Quaking, or fire from God. . . . If I have found
This grove, for sure some wingèd guide from you
Hath led me. How else had I trod so true,
Grey-souled to your all-wineless house, and won
My rest with you on this unchiselled stone?
O Spirits, by Apollo's word I pray,
Vouchsafe me, after so long life, some way
To pass and make an end, unless ye know
Of aught that lacketh still to the great woe
This heart must bear, beyond all human kind.
Sweet Maidens born of Darkness old and blind,
Be near, be merciful; O thou, alone
Of cities, whom God's Virgin calls her own,
Precious beyond all cities, hear me; scan
The shape of this dim shadow, once a man
And Oedipus . . . but I was different then.

ANTIGONE

Peace, Father, now! I see some aged men
Here hasting, to spy out thy resting place.

OEDIPUS

I am silent. . . . Hide me from the path a space
Behind yon trees, to hearken what they say.
Some knowledge of their minds would ease our way.

[ANTIGONE *leads* OEDIPUS *into the Grove*
where he stays unseen.

24

Enter CHORUS *of Elders, in groups, searching.*

CHORUS

[*Various voices, confusedly.*

Strophe. —Mark there! Who was it?—Where lieth
   he? Fled, is he?—Gone as a quick
   bird goes?

—The daring of it! The daring of it! But
   use your eyes. Sweep the thicket
   clear.

—Put question to everyone. Old and a
   wanderer?—Surely a wanderer; no
   man that knows,

Would dare to harbour him here;

Here in the trackless grove
Of Them with whom none may strive,
The Virgins who know not love,
And their fear is a thing alive;
We dare not name their name,
We raise no eyes to them;
Only a prayer, a spell
We whisper beneath our breath,
A voiceless wordless thought;
And a man is here, men tell,
Whom no fear entereth!

LEADER

Yet I see him not,

Nor mark nor sign of him, though all round
Mine eyes have searched thro' the holy ground.

25

OEDIPUS   [*From the Grove.*

Behold the man ye desire.
In sound are mine only eyes.

LEADER

Ah! Awful voice, and dire
Aspect!

OEDIPUS

But yet nowise
A lawbreaker!

LEADER

God's mercy!
What can this old man be?

OEDIPUS

Not one of a lot so bright,
 Ye guards: not a man to bless:
Who walks by another's sight,
Groping, and all his might
 Anchored on feebleness.

CHORUS   [*Confusedly.*

Antistrophe. —Ah there! His eyes, they are visionless!
   Was it then ever so? Even from
   birth?
  —A bitter lifetime, a long long lifetime
   is written there. Yet, if I can
   aid,

26

Thou shalt not add sin to thy sorrows,
O Stranger. For this is great
trespass! The wrath of the
earth
Lies in that speechless glade,

Where the grass is green below,
And rock-cupped waters flow
With offerings honey-sweet
Blended . . . Ah back! Thy feet
Back there! And speak not yet.

[*He moves a step or two out.*

LEADER

Back still. It is safer there.
Dost hear me, thou desolate,
Thou age-worn wanderer?
Out from the precinct, nearer still
Where the ground is free. Then speak thy will.

OEDIPUS   [*Hesitating.*

My child, what can one think?

ANTIGONE

Incline
Thy will, Father, to these men's will.

OEDIPUS   [*Assenting.*

Give me thy hand.

ANTIGONE

'Tis laid in thine.

OEDIPUS

I come.—Oh, bring me not to ill,
Strangers, because I trusted you
And did as ye would have me do.

LEADER

No man shall move thee more. No man
Shall break thy rest or show thee wrath.

OEDIPUS

Further?

LEADER

Yes.

OEDIPUS

Further?

LEADER

Still a span:
Thou lead him: thou canst see the path.

[*To* ANTIGONE.

There, 'tis enough.

OEDIPUS

Now may I sit?

LEADER

Aye; crouch a little: at thy right
The rock's edge . . .

ANTIGONE

I will show thee it.

OEDIPUS
[*Seating himself on the Rock seat.*

Oh, without hope or sight!

LEADER

Unhappy one, now thou hast ease again,
Say who thou art, thus woman-led in pain;
What is thy fatherland?

OEDIPUS   [*Desperately.*

I have no land . . .
And now, no further!

LEADER

I scarce understand.

OEDIPUS

Ask me not who I am, nor strive nor seek . . .

LEADER

What can this mean?

OEDIPUS

Dark is my race . . .

LEADER   [*Sternly.*

Come, speak!

OEDIPUS

My child, what shall I say?

LEADER

                    Speak swiftly thou!
Thy lineage and thy father's name!

OEDIPUS

                    Woe's me,
What will become of us?

ANTIGONE

                    Best face them now
And speak; we are on the edge of destiny.

OEDIPUS

Then speak I will; Strangers, I have no way
To hide it more . . .

LEADER

Ye both make long delay.

OEDIPUS

Ye know by fame one born of Laius . . .

CHORUS   [*Confusedly.*

O God!

OEDIPUS

. . . a Prince of the Labdacidae,

CHORUS   [*In tumult.*

Great God in heaven!

OEDIPUS

. . . the ill-starred Oedipus?

CHORUS

God shield us! *Thou* art he?

VARIOUS VOICES   [*Confused.*

O horror beyond horror!——Get thee gone!
Hated of God!——Out, out, accursèd one!

OEDIPUS

Fear not the words I speak . . .

31

CHORUS

—Thou bleeding stain,
Thou sin incarnate!

OEDIPUS (to ANTIGONE)

Child, what will they do?

CHORUS

—Out from the land! Begone for ever, both!
—Out from the land!

OEDIPUS

Ye gave but now your oath . . .

CHORUS

—Go, go! And far from Athens . . . both the twain!

OEDIPUS

. . . Will ye not prove it true?

CHORUS   [*various voices.*

—No; you deceived us first. Ye did a worse
    Wrong. Tis no sin to pay thee back in kind . . .
—Shall we give faith and kindness for the curse
    Ye have cast on us?—Thou evil thing and blind,
Speak not but go! We have no rest for thee
In Athens. Go thy ways and leave her free!
    [OEDIPUS, *his voice drowned, loses heart and gives
        way:* ANTIGONE *stands before him.*

32

ANTIGONE

O pitying strangers, since ye will not hear
My old blind father, for some tales ye have heard
Of his unpurposed sin, Oh, still give ear
To a lost maiden, and accept the word
I speak for his sake . . . See, I am not blind
As he is. I can look into your eyes;
Look into mine! 'Tis one of your own kind
Implores you for compassion. Our life lies
In your hand, as in heaven's . . . Unbend that brow
And grant the prayer we scarce dare hope for now.

Oh, if there be at home one thing you love
Most, I beseech you in the name thereof,
Be it woman, be it child, or work or God,
I that have nothing! And before you hate
My father, think what man can fly the road
      That God hath marked and Fate.

LEADER

Daughter of Oedipus, both him and thee
We pity in this strange calamity.
Yet if he stay, on all our land we dread
God's wrath for harboured sin.—Our word is said.

OEDIPUS
      [*Who has recovered himself.*

What good is in men's praise? What profiteth
High rumour, rolling like an idle breath?

In fame is Athens the most god-fearing
Of cities; only she is swift to bring
Help to the stranger vexèd, only she
Strong to defend the weak. . . . Are you for me
That Athens? Who have brought me here, beguiled
From refuge, and then hunt me to the wild
In dread at my mere name? For sure 'tis not
Myself ye fear, nor any deed I wrought . . .
If deeds ye call what were more sufferings
Than doings . . .

     Since ye make me speak the things
Ye dread me for, my parents, and the whole
Darkness, how dare ye call me in my soul
Evil? They planned my death: I smote again
My smiters. Was that sin? Nay, had my brain
Seen all my hand was working, even so
'Twere no great sin. As things were, each dark blow
I struck, was struck unknowing, but those two
Who cast their child to death, they knew, they knew!

Oh, in God's name, I charge you, since 'tis ye
None else, have drawn me from this sanctuary,
Be now yourselves mine altar. Nor be hot
To help the Gods with wrath. They need it not.
They know the innocent and they know the man
Of sin, and never since this world began
Hath wrong escaped them and gone free. Let Them
Suffice for me, nor cloud the diadem
Of blessèd Athens by this traitor's deed.

        [*To the* LEADER.

O thou who didst accept me in my need,
Be true! Save me and keep! Nor, quailing now
To see the wreck and horror of this brow,
Cast me away. Both god-fearing am I
And altar-sacred, and a boon most high
I bring your people. When there cometh he
Who needs must come, your King, whoe'er he be,
Then ye shall hearken and know all; till then,
Do me no wrong.

LEADER

O ancient among men,
I needs must bow before thy counsel, thus
In grave words uttered. It sufficeth us
To leave thee judgeless 'till the King be come.

OEDIPUS

Where dwells your king?

LEADER

He keeps his father's home,
The fortress of our land. A messenger,
The same who found me, went to seek him there.

OEDIPUS

Think ye himself will come? Hath a king's mind
Room for the call of one so poor and blind?

LEADER

For sure he will. Thou hast far-reaching fame
In Greece, old man, and once he hears thy name,
Though sleeping, he would wake and hither speed.

OEDIPUS

Pray heaven, he come, to serve his city's need
And mine! His own true welfare he must seek.

ANTIGONE   [*Looking off*

O Zeus! How dare I think it? Dare I speak?

OEDIPUS

What is it, child Antigone?

ANTIGONE

     I see
A damsel on a colt of Sicily,
Her hat broad-shaded to the sun; apace
She rides to us. I cannot see her face . . .
Is it or is it not? I lose my way
Thinking; yes; no. I know not what to say.
Ah, she dismounts. . . . She has waved to me and smiled!
Father! It is Ismênê.

OEDIPUS

     How, my child?
What sayst thou?

Antigone

Tis thy daughter and mine own
Sister. Her voice . . . Ah, thou wilt know its tone.

Ismene   [*Entering*.

O Father! Sister! Names so sweet of sound,
How hardly have I found you! And when found
I scarce can see you for these blinding tears.

Oedipus

Child, thou art come!

Ismene

O Father, how the years
Have wrecked thee!

Oedipus

Thou art with us?

Ismene

And some pain
It cost me.

Oedipus

Touch me, child.

Ismene

To both the twain
I reach my hands.   [*All three clasp hands*

37

OEDIPUS

O sisters true to me!

ISMENE

Alas, what suffering, suffering, lives!

OEDIPUS   That she

And I must lead?

ISMENE

And I because of you.

OEDIPUS

Why hast thou come?

ISMENE

To give thee service true.

OEDIPUS

Thou hast longed to see me?

ISMENE

I had news for thee,

And came myself to bring it secretly

With this one faithful thrall to guide my way.

OEDIPUS

The young strong men, thy brothers, where are they?

ISMENE

They! They are where they are; and dire their state.

OEDIPUS

Those two! 'Tis said, in Egypt the men wait
At home in comfort, sitting at the loom
Indoors, while out abroad the women roam,
Toiling to earn their bread. 'Tis so with you
My daughters. They whose place it was to do
These deeds, like girls at home will stay at ease
While you two in their stead go forth to appease
Your father's sufferings. This one, from the day
She ceased to be a child and won her way
Towards womanhood, hath ever been my guide,
The old man's staff. She has wandered through the wide
Forests; aye, often hungry, with bare feet,
She has trod through wintry rain and scorching heat.
She thought not of the ease and royal fare
At home, could but her father have due care.
And thou, child, camest forth in former days
From Thebes to let me know by secret ways
All oracles that touched my destiny.
A faithful watcher, Child, I had in thee,
When first they drove me from the land. But now
What brings thee to this place? What comest thou
To tell me? For I trow not empty here
Thou comest, nor without some load of fear.

ISMENE

I will not tell what dangers of the road
Befell me, searching for the unknown abode
That covered thee. Why should I wake again
By a tale told those memories of pain?
But thine ill-fated sons: 'tis of the fell
Doom that besets those two, I came to tell.
At first they were content thy throne should be
Passed on to Creon; that alone would free
Thebes from her stain, so thought they, pondering
What ancient poisons to thy lineage cling.
Then, or by act of god, or by their own
Wild hearts, between those brothers twain was sown
A seed of strife—O thrice-infatuate!—
To grasp again at power and kingly state.
Now, in hot youth, the second of the pair
Hath ta'en from Polynîces, the true heir,
His crown and right, and cast him from the land.
He fled, as now in Thebes the rumours stand,
To hill-girt Argos: there, though poor and lost,
Won the king's daughter; won an armèd host
To swear that Argos now, as his ally,
Shall lay Thebes low or lift her to the sky
In glory. 'Tis not words; deeds terrible
Are gathering here, Father. And who can tell
What gods may yet have pity for thy fall?

OEDIPUS

Hadst thou that hope? How should the gods at all
Have thought for me, to raise me ere I die!

ISMENE

What gives me hope is their last prophecy.

OEDIPUS

An oracle, my child? What hath it said?

ISMENE

That thou beyond all else, alive or dead,
Shalt be desired of Thebes, if Thebes would live.

OEDIPUS

Live? What life is there such as I could give?

ISMENE

The secret health of Thebes is lodged in thee.

OEDIPUS

I am nothing; who can make a man of me?

ISMENE

The gods o'erthrew thee, they can raise thee too.

OEDIPUS

Raise, weak with age, whom young and strong they
        threw?

ISMENE

Creon himself believes that word of fate.
He is travelling here himself and will not wait.

41

OEDIPUS

Explain, my child. What seeks he by such toil?

ISMENE

To have thy body not in Theban soil
But in their grasp, close by the border laid.

OEDIPUS

Beyond their gates, how can I bring them aid?

ISMENE

Thy tomb, left in neglect, would work them woe.

OEDIPUS

That much without god's warning they might know.

ISMENE

For fear of that they fain would bury thee
Within their own control, not leave thee free.

OEDIPUS

Some Theban dust they will give to wrap me in?

ISMENE

That is forbid thee by thine ancient sin.

OEDIPUS

Then never shall they hold me in their power!

ISMENE

Woe, then to Thebes, when comes the appointed hour!

OEDIPUS

What visitation, child, shall bring their doom?

ISMENE

Thine anger, when their feet shall tread thy tomb.

OEDIPUS

From whose word, daughter, is this presage known?

ISMENE

From sacred envoys to the Delphic throne.

OEDIPUS

'Tis truly of me, Apollo hath spoken thus?

ISMENE

'Tis thus the word from Delphi came to us.

OEDIPUS

Hath either of my sons that message heard?

ISMENE

Both; they have pondered well Apollo's word.

OEDIPUS

False-hearted sons! Their rank and royalty
Were more to them than any thoughts of me.

ISMENE

I grieve to hear such words, yet hear I must,

OEDIPUS

Then quench not, O ye gods, if gods are just,
Their fore-ordainèd strife! And be it mine
This issue to decide, which now they join,
Spear against spear, in never-ending hate;
Then neither shall that man abide in state
Who now sits crowned, nor he that is cast out
Ever return. They spoke not, hindered not,
They stood and saw their father, driven in shame
From land and home, with heralds to proclaim
His everlasting exile. Wilt thou say
'Twas then mine own wish to be cast away,
And Thebes but granted what I asked? Not so.
On that first day, when all my soul, I know,
Was fiery with self-loathing, death alone
Seemed kind, the sinner's death by stone on stone.
None then stood forth to give me my desire.
But after, when, with length of days, the fire
Was burnt out, and I grew to know that wrath
Had swept me away upon too wild a path,
Too fierce a judgement of an old misdeed,
Twas then, then, after years, that Thebes decreed

My banishment; and they, born of my blood,
Sons, in a father's peril, when they could
Have helped me would not, till for lack of one
Slight word I was cast out, beggared, alone,
Till death; save only that these sisters, two
Young girls, with what of strength they had, were true;
Came with me, found the food I live by, made
The earth no longer dreadful to my tread.
My only kindred these; these gave me love.
But those two sons—so hear me Zeus above!—
Who sold their father for a royal seat
And sceptre, and Thebes bowing at their feet,
My voice shall save them not, nor shall my throne
Bring blessing. That I know, and long have known
By ancient voices that long since have rolled
About me, and the tale this maid hath told.
Bid them send out their trackers—Creon, yea,
And what so traitor else in Thebes hath sway,
Will ye but take me in, will ye but stand
With These, the Holy Ones who watch your land,
Athens hath here a well-spring from which flows
Strong help for her and downfall to her foes.

LEADER

Most worthy art thou, Oedipus, of all
Compassion, thou and these two maids withal;
And more, we ponder on that secret vow
Of help through thee to Athens. Therefore now
I fain would give thee warning for thy weal.

OEDIPUS

Friend, speak thy warning. I will all fulfil.

LEADER

Make offering to these Spirits, to whose ground
Thou first hast come, and crossed their holy bound.

OEDIPUS

What is the ritual, Stranger? Let me know.

LEADER

First, from a fountain of unfailing flow
Draughts must be poured by hands without a stain.

OEDIPUS

By stainless hands? And when the draught is ta'en?

LEADER

Great urns, an artist's work, are there; all down
The edge and the two handles weave a crown.

OEDIPUS

A crown of wool, or green leaves, or what kind?

LEADER

A young lamb's fleece about it should be twined.

Oedipus

So be it; and after——how complete the rite?

Leader

Pour with thy face set toward the rising light.

Oedipus

Into those crownèd urns the gift is poured?

Leader

Three times; the vessel emptied at the third.

Oedipus

How should I fill it? Make that also clear.

Leader

With water and honey; let no wine be near.

Oedipus

And when the shadowed Earth has drunk my gift?

Leader

In both thine arms branches of olive lift
Thrice nine, and laying them, thy prayer recite:

Oedipus

Speak it. That prayer must be a charm of might.

47

LEADER

As they are called The Merciful, beseech
That now they will a hand of mercy reach
To save their suppliant; let that prayer be said
By thee, or whoso speaketh in thy stead,
With un-uplifted voice and speech unheard;
Then go, and look not back. In every word
Do thus, and I beside thee joyfully
Will stand; else, stranger, I should fear for thee.

OEDIPUS

Daughters, ye heard what these near-dwellers say?

ISMENE

We heard. Give us thy charge and we obey.

OEDIPUS

I can not go. A twofold plague on me
Is laid, who have no strength and cannot see.
Go, one of you, then, and perform the rite.
The prayer of one pure heart, I think, hath might
To atone for many. Let what must be done
Be done with speed. But leave me not alone
The while. My body scarce hath power to stand
Friendless, or move without some guiding hand.

ISMENE

I will perform the rite. But will ye not
Direct me, strangers, to the appointed spot?

LEADER

'Tis in this grove, but at the further side;
And if thou hast need of aught, there is a guide
Keeping the shrine, who will advise with thee.

ISMENE

So, to my task. And thou, Antigone,
Watch o'er our father. Toiling for his sake
An aching body thinks not of the ache.

[*Exit* ISMENE.

CHORUS

Strophe.
It were cruel to awaken into life an ancient anguish
  That hath long been untroubled in its rest,
Yet I long to ask . . .

OEDIPUS

What ask ye?

CHORUS

  Of the sick wound beyond healing,
That hath all, all, the life of thee opprest.

OEDIPUS

Ah, unveil not to the sunlight the long shame that I
  have suffered,
  I pray thee; grant so much to a guest.

49   D

CHORUS

Tis a tale spread wide and never ceasing,
        And I fain would know the truth.

OEDIPUS

                                Woe is me!

CHORUS

Thou wilt bear with us, I pray thee.

OEDIPUS

                Woe is me!

CHORUS

                                Nay, I beseech thee
        Give grace to me as I gave to thee.

OEDIPUS

Antistrophe.

I have borne a yoke of evil that I willed not, God be
        witness!
        Not one step I purposed of the way.

CHORUS

What evil?

OEDIPUS

                To a bondage of great sin the City bound me,
        They bound me on their high bridal day.

CHORUS

'Twas a mother, though that name can scarce be spoken,
They delivered to thine arms, so men say.

OEDIPUS

Woe is me, 'tis death to hear it! Ye have spoke the
word, O strangers;
And these twain that in my darkness I begot . . .

CHORUS

Ah, what wilt thou?

OEDIPUS

My two daughters, two destroyers . . .

CHORUS

God in heaven!

OEDIPUS

On a mother's flesh were wrought.

CHORUS

Strophe 2.
Then these are both thy children and . . .

OEDIPUS

The very sisters of their sire.

CHORUS

Oh, horror!

51

OEDIPUS

Horrors beyond count
Come sweeping on my soul, like fire.

CHORUS

Thou hast suffered!

OEDIPUS

Yes, I have suffered; pangs
Are mine that never sleep nor tire.

CHORUS

Thou hast done . . .

OEDIPUS

I did no deed!

CHORUS

No deed?

OEDIPUS

I took a gift the City gave.
Oh, why should she have given me that,
The City that I sought to save?

CHORUS

Antistrophe.
Unhappy! Blood, too, on thy hand!

OEDIPUS

What wouldst thou? What dost seek to know?

CHORUS

A father's blood.

OEDIPUS

Thou seekest still
Torture on torture, blow on blow!

CHORUS

Didst thou not slay?

OEDIPUS

I slew. But there
Mine innocent heart hath answer, too.

CHORUS

What answer?

OEDIPUS

'Twas but Justice.

CHORUS

How?

OEDIPUS

'Tis simply told. The man I slew
Would have slain me. In will, in law,
Unstained I did what I must do.

LEADER

See, at thy call, King Theseus, Aigeus' son,
Cometh himself; thy prayer will now be won.

[*Enter* THESEUS.

THESEUS

I know thee, Child of Laïus. Legendwise
The blood-dark desolation of thine eyes
Hath reached my ears, and here being come to-day
Thou hast made thy tale more clear. This wild array
And grief-dishonoured brow suffice to prove
Thou art that King indeed, and needs must move
Our pity. Say what now can comfort thee.
What ask ye of my city or of me,
Thou and thy most sad helper? 'Twere a dire
Task that should make me shrink from your desire,
Who well remember how myself, a child,
Bore exile like to thine, and peril piled
On peril fronted on strange shores alone,
Which no man else hath borne. Therefore from none
Who walks, like thee, in travail on strange ground
Will I avert mine eyes. Here, standing crowned,
I know my lot is mortal and for me
Abides no surer morrow than for thee.

OEDIPUS

Theseus, thy nobleness in little speech
Hath saved me long discourse. No need to teach
My name to thee nor country, nor the race
I spring from. All thou knowest. One sole grace
I have to ask thee and my tale is told.

Theseus

So be it. I fain would hear.

Oedipus [*After a slight pause*

Theseus, this old
And grief-worn body as a gift I bear
To Athens and to thee; not passing fair
To human eyes, yet 'tis a precious thing.

Theseus

How precious, friend? What blessing will it bring?

Oedipus

Hereafter thou shalt learn, not now. Not now.

Theseus

At what time shall we feel it? Knowest thou?

Oedipus

When I am dead and thou hast made my grave.

Theseus

Nay! Is it Time's last bounty thou wilt crave,
With all between uncared for or forgot?

Oedipus

Give me the last: the rest shall fail me not.

THESEUS

Full gladly I would grant some larger grace.

OEDIPUS

Think! think! 'Tis no light trial thou shalt face.

THESEUS

How? Will thy sons some blame against me bring?

OEDIPUS

They seek to take me back to Thebes, O King.

THESEUS

In kindness? Then 'twere ill to stay exiled.

OEDIPUS

When I craved home they drove me to the wild.

THESEUS

Proud heart! Small help is, in affliction, pride.

OEDIPUS

Wait. E'er thou hast heard all, forbear to chide.

THESEUS

Say on. I must not judge before I know.

OEDIPUS

Long have I suffered, woe on deadly woe . . .

THESEUS

What wouldst thou tell? That ancient tale of blood?

OEDIPUS

Nay; that tale everywhere is understood:
This is another. I am cast away
By mine own folk from mine own land, and may
Never return nor dwell with them again.
My father's blood hath left too deep a stain.

THESEUS

How can they call thee home, being thus shut out?

OEDIPUS   [*Mysteriously.*

The mouth of God shall compass them about.

THESEUS

With dread of some foreshadowed misery?

OEDIPUS

That in this land, unless preserved by me,
Thebes shall be smitten and perish.

THESEUS

All is peace
'Twixt Thebes and me. How should that comfort cease?

OEDIPUS

Fair Aigeus' son, only to gods on high
Not to grow old is given, nor yet to die,
All else is turmoiled by our master, Time.
Decay is in earth's bloom and manhood's prime,
Faith dies and Unfaith blossoms like a flower,
And who of men shall find from hour to hour,
Or in loud cities and the marts thereof,
Or silent chambers of his own heart's love,
One wind blow true for ever? Soon or late
Hate shall be love and love veer back to hate.
And now if summer shines and all is well
'Twixt Thebes and thee, lo, Time immeasurable
Flows on, night after night, day after day,
Till that day come when Thebes, in armed array,
Raging for some slight cause, shall front you here
And this fair concord scatter with the spear.
Then, here beneath them, my wrongèd body, deep
And cold, shall turn him in his starvèd sleep
And drain the hot red blood of them, like dew,
If God be still God and his Son speak true . . .

But who would breathe the secrets of the dark?
I end as I began. Do thou but mark
My promise and thine own, and none shall say
That Theseus on a false and wasted day

Did welcome Oedipus beneath these skies
To dwell for ever more . . . unless God lies.

LEADER

Sire, from the first, sure-seeming promises
He hath made to Athens, these and like to these.

THESEUS

Who would reject the hand of such a man?
Have not his fathers shared, since Thebes began,
Our hearth in sojourn and our arms in war?
And he, by men cast off and driven afar,
Hath none save God and me; from such an one
Cometh great vengeance or great benison.
I will not spurn his prayer nor cast away
The boon of his good will. . . . Be thou this day
Our citizen.

> [*He clasps* OEDIPUS' *hand.* OEDIPUS *much moved
> cannot at first answer.*

        Stay, if it pleasure thee,
Here under these men's care; or come with me
To mine own house. Have it which way thou please.

OEDIPUS

O Zeus, be merciful to men like these!

THESEUS

Which wouldst thou, then? Wilt share my hearth and
    cheer?

OEDIPUS

If that might be . . . ! But no. The place is here.

THESEUS

The place? For what? I will not hinder thee.

OEDIPUS

Where I shall break them that rejected me.

THESEUS

If that could be, 'twere great,

OEDIPUS

    It shall be, friend,
If but thy word stay faithful to the end.

THESEUS

Fear not. I shall not fail thee.

OEDIPUS

    'Tis enough.
I would not, like a man of slighter stuff,
Bind thee with oaths.

THESEUS

    'Twould bring no surer trust.

OEDIPUS

How wilt thou act, then?

THESEUS

What dost fear the most?

OEDIPUS

Those men will come , . .

THESEUS

In these men's care thou art.

OEDIPUS

And if thou leave me . . .

THESEUS

Teach me not my part!

OEDIPUS

'Tis fear constrains me.

THESEUS

I know naught of fear.

OEDIPUS

Thou knowest not their threats.

THESEUS

I know, from here

No man in my despite shall carry thee.
These threats; how often in some ecstasy
Of wrath men rage in stormy words and vain!
But when the true mind is enthroned again

61

All is forgot. These men who wax so bold
In wrath, and swear to tear thee from my hold,
May find, I think, before such heights they scale,
A sundering sea too wide, too hard to sail.
Thou needst not me. If Lord Apollo here
Hath led thee, here canst sojourn without fear;
Howbeit, the name of Theseus, though his arm
Be distant, shall safeguard thee from all harm.

[*Exit* THESEUS.

CHORUS

Here, where the Warrior Steed had birth,
    Come, wanderer, to a place of rest,
A home, the dearest upon earth,
    Beneath Colonus' gleaming crest.
Often a secret music through this vale
Comes thrilling, where some sweet-voiced nightingale
    Hides in a dell of green;
She loves the clustering ivy, dark as wine,
And that deep-leaved, that thousand-berried shrine,
Where no foot treads, where never sun may shine
    Nor storm-wind pierce the screen.
Only the mystic Dionysus there,
Ringed by the nymphs who erst his cradle bare,
    Treadeth his dance unseen.

Here blossoms in fresh dew from heaven
    The crocus with its gleam of gold,
And clusters of narcissus, given
    As crowns by men of old

To Maid and Mother, goddesses most high;
Nor ever run those sleepless channels dry
 Which shepherd o'er the plain
The runlets of Cephîsus; day by day
Through earth's deep bosom he will wind his way,
And swift her life increaseth, whereso stray
 Those waters without stain;
A haunt not hated by the Muses' band,
Nor turneth Aphrodîtê from this land
 Averse her golden rein.

One bloom I know is hers, which hath no peer
In Asian lands nor Pelops' Dorian isle.
A thing self-born, a dread to the hostile spear,
 Fearless of force or guile,
Whose root most richly in this soil hath sprung,
The gray-leaved Olive, nurse of all things young;
Which nor the craft of age nor youth's wild will
With ravishing hand shall conquer; orbed on high
Zeus of the Olive guards her still, and still
 Flashes Athena's eye.

And one last praise I utter o'er this land,
Our Mother; 'tis a gift to her alone
Set out by Cronos-born Poseidon's hand,
 Who raised her to this throne,
And made her mistress of his secrets three,
The Horses, the Young Horses, and the Sea.

The Horse he gave; the Curb that maketh sweet
Its wildness on our ways; the Oar he gave
Deft to man's hand, fast following o'er the wave
    The Nereids' hundred feet.

ANTIGONE   [*Looking off.*

O land by all men's praises richly blest,
Now shall thy shining honour meet the test.

OEDIPUS

Daughter, what is it?

ANTIGONE

      Father, hitherward
Creon is coming, Creon with his guard.

OEDIPUS

O Elders, if you love me, 'tis in you
Alone that I may find deliverance true!

LEADER

Fear not. It shall be thine. Though I be frayed
With age, the strength of Athens doth not fade.
        [*Enter* CREON *with armed guards*

CRÈON

Ye gentle habitants, do I surmise
A sudden trouble clouding in your eyes

64

At my approach? Nay, prithee, put all dread
Away, and let no word of wrath be said.
'Tis not in any mood for violent deeds
I come, an old man, to a land which leads
All Hellas in renown and majesty,
To beg this wanderer to return with me,
Two aged Thebans, home to Thebes again.
Not my sole voice, but every citizen
Through me doth call him, seeing that I, in race
His nearest, suffer most for his distress.

O Oedipus unhappy, hear my call:
Come to thy home. The sons of Cadmus all
Pray thee with right, but none with right so great
As mine, who most for thy forlorn estate
—Were I not else the vilest of mankind?—
Feel pain, old friend, whom on strange soil I find
For ever wandering, lacking all, thine aid
In travel none, alas, but this one maid.
Poor girl, whom never I had thought to see
Fallen like this to shame and misery;
Her only care thee and thy wounded face;
Begging her food; so young, a husbandless
Virgin, a prey to every passer by!

Ah, shame upon me! 'Tis a wrong most high
'Gainst thee, 'gainst me, 'gainst all our house and pride!
I have named it: 'tis a thing too gross to hide.
Oh, by our fathers' gods, sweep it away,
Thou, Oedipus, and grant me what I pray,
Consenting to come with me to thine own
Land, to thy fathers' house. All love be shown

65   E

To Athens: she is worthy: but more worth
Is home, thy home which fostered thee from birth.

OEDIPUS

Man, wilt thou shrink from nothing? Canst devise
Always a fair front built by subtle lies?
Dost hope to cheat me still; trap me again
In snares whose memory is my bitterest pain?
In the early days when, sick with mine own sin,
I prayed to be cast out, to hold me in
And thwart my longing was thy whole intent;
But when my fury of self-rage was spent
And sweet it seemed in mine own house to stay
Sheltered, then thou must have me thrust away
From home, from country; little to thy mind
Was then all this regard for kith and kind.
And now again, when thou hast found me here
Well-friended in this city and held dear
By her strong sons, thy one thought is to part
Me from her, by soft words from a hard heart.
How should it please me, thus, against my mood
And will, by them I love not to be wooed?
If one when thou wert starving brought no aid,
But after, when all hunger was allayed,
Lavished his graceless meats, would that not be
A vain thing? That is what thou bringst to me;
Soft promises with bitter deeds behind!
Come, I will speak and show these friends what kind
Of man thou art. In love thou comest now
To lead me to mine own old home? Not thou!

66

Thou com'st to lay my dead bones in a grave
Beyond thy borders, that their spell may save
Thy land for ever from the invader's tread.
That thou shalt never have! I grant instead
Deep in thy soil, rooted eternally,
My curse; and to my two sons I decree
My land ... enough to die in! ... Is it I
Or thou more surely knoweth what things lie
In store for Thebes? 'Tis I, not thou, have heard
The surer message, even Apollo's word,
Which errs not, being the word of Zeus, his sire.
Thy lips are as a sword engaged for hire
And sharpened; but the use of it will wreak
More ill than good to them that bade thee speak.
But go. I know I cannot move thee. Go,
And leave me here, outcast ... Aye, even so
I am content, so but I have my will.

CREON

Dost think thy wild words bring to me more ill
Than to thyself, man, in our converse now?

OEDIPUS

I only pray that on my misery thou
Mayst have no power, nor yet on these men's ears.

CREON

Unhappy man, not yet, for all thy years,
Grown wise! Should age be so self-torturing?

OEDIPUS

That subtle tongue! No honest man can bring
The self-same art to plead for good or ill.

CREON

Words may be many and yet lack all skill.

OEDIPUS

And thine, so brief, are certain of their aim?

CREON

With minds like thine, that were a hopeless claim.

OEDIPUS

Go! For these too I speak. Go, nor beset
With spies this land, my home predestinate.

CREON

These men, not thou, can say what answer vain
Thou hast made to kindness. Once I have thee ta'en . . .

OEDIPUS

Ta'en! Who can take me against these men's will?

CREON

So be it! . . . Yet I can make thee miserable.

OEDIPUS

These threats . . . what base have they, or what intent?

68

CREON

Thou hast two daughters. One I have seized and sent
To Thebes. The other I shall take anon.

OEDIPUS

Woe's me!

CREON

Thou soon shalt have good cause to moan.

OEDIPUS

Thou hast ta'en my child!

CREON

And soon shall have them both.

OEDIPUS

Friends! Friends! What say you? Will you keep your
oath?
Oh, cast from Athens this ungodly man!

LEADER

Stranger, begone! Unlawful is the plan
Thou plottest—and unlawful thy deeds done.

CREON   [*To the Guards.*

'Tis time, men. Seize the girl there. Get her gone
Quickly. Use force if she will not obey.

ANTIGONE

Where can I go? What succour can I pray
From god or man?

LEADER

Stranger, what deeds are these?

CREON

I touch not him. 'Tis my own ward I seize.

OEDIPUS

Elders of Athens!

LEADER

Man, a deed thou hast done
'Gainst law . . .

CREON

Most lawful!

LEADER

How?

CREON

I claim my own.

OEDIPUS

Strophe.
O Athens!

LEADER

Wouldst thou so?
Back, stranger   Set her free.
Shall it be word or blow?

CREON

Hands off, man!

LEADER

Not from thee,
Not while such things can be!

CREON

Touch me and Thebes in arms shall join the fray.

OEDIPUS

I warned you. . .

LEADER

I command you, set her free!

CREON

Give orders where thou hast authority.

LEADER

Let go, I charge you!

CREON

Captain, go your way.

71

CHORUS

Forward! Oh, forward here,
　　Ye who about us dwell!
Forward! They wrong our dear
　　Athens, our citadel
　　By force. Oh, guard her well!

ANTIGONE

Woe's me! They are dragging me. O strangers,
　　friends . . .

OEDIPUS

Where art thou, child?

ANTIGONE

　　　　I am torn away from thee.

OEDIPUS

Thy hand, my child!

ANTIGONE

　　　　I cannot move my hands.

CREON

Away with her!

OEDIPUS

　　　Misery, misery!
　　　　　EXEUNT *Soldiers with* ANTIGONE

CREON

So those two loving crutches shall no more
Support thy goings! 'Tis thy will to score
A victory o'er thy kindred and thy state,
Whose servant, I, their king, am designate?
Enjoy thy victory! Thou shalt learn at last
Thy lesson, that both now and in time past
A fool thou hast been to spurn all well-wishers
And have no guide but rage, thy lifelong curse.

LEADER

Hold, stranger! Stay!

CREON

　　　　　I warn thee; drop that arm.

LEADER

I will not, till those maids are safe from harm.

CREON

A greater forfeit then shall Athens pay
Than those two girls. I seek a larger prey.

LEADER

What mean'st thou?

CREON

　　　　　This blind man shall follow too.

73

LEADER

Thou threatenest us?

CREON

And what I threaten do.

LEADER

Not if the Prince of Athens hinders thee!

OEDIPUS

That pitiless voice! Wilt thou lay hands on me?

CREON

Be silent, thou!

OEDIPUS

O grant me, of your grace,
Voice, even here, ye spirits of this place,
To speak one curse! Thou cruellest of men,
Mine eyes of old being darkened, hast thou then
My one light, my true eye, unshielded, torn
By violence from me? Therefore, be it sworn!
The all-seeing Sun on thee and all thy line
Shall bring to pass . . . an old age such as mine!

CREON

Ye see his madness, people of the land?

OEDIPUS

They see both me and thee, and understand,
To what deeds I retort with empty breath.

CREON

By force then, for I will not curb my wrath,
Alone here as I am and old and slow,
Myself will seize him.

OEDIPUS

Woe upon thee, woe!

CHORUS

Antistrophe.

Stranger, a boldness rare
Is thine if such a thought
Thou darest.

CREON

See! I dare.

CHORUS

Are Athens' laws as naught?

CREON

Weakness can master strength when justice leads.

OEDIPUS

Ye hear his words?

LEADER

Which never shall be deeds!
Zeus knoweth!

CREON

Zeus may know, not thou for sure!

LEADER

This is an outrage.

CREON

One you must endure.

CHORUS

Hither, ye people all!
   'Tis crime, and more than crime.
Lords of the land, I call
   For succour, for help in time!
              [*Enter* THESEUS.

THESEUS

What means that cry? What work is here? What fear
   hath made you summon me
From the high Altar where I stood in prayer to Him
   who Rules the Sea,
The Lord of your Colonus? Speak and tarry not; let
   all be said;
For hot-foot, recking not of ease or order, to your call
   I sped.

76

OEDIPUS

O faithful friend, tis thou! Thy voice I know.
This man hath wronged me, struck me a coward's blow.

THESEUS

What kind of wrong? And who hath wrought it? Say.

OEDIPUS

Yon Creon, whom thou seest, hath torn away
Both, both, those that are left to me, and fled.

THESEUS

What means he?

OEDIPUS

What I have suffered I have said.

THESEUS   [*To his attendants.*

Up, with all speed! Go, take mine order straight
To yonder altars where my people wait.
Break off the sacrifice. Bid foot and horse
Uncurbed, together, speed to where the course
Of the two trackways joins, lest they get past
Our border watch unseen, and I be cast
To scorn as one by strangers easily
Despoiled and mocked at. Up, I tell thee; fly!
For this man, if mine anger ranged as far
As his offences, not without a scar
Had he escaped my grasp. But, as it is,
On him my sentence shall be even as his

On those two maids . . . Thou art my prisoner here,
And shalt not move till thou restore them, clear
And free before mine eyes. The deed thou hast done
Is worthy neither of me nor of thine own
City nor race. Thou hast trespassed on a land
Observing justice, firm to take her stand
Always on law; rushed in and, hot with pride,
Swept all the City's' stablished powers aside;
Ta'en prisoners at thy pleasure; laid thine hand
On all that pleased thee. Is Athens then a land
Of slaves, not men, and I a thing of naught?
Thebes, surely, to such doings schooled thee not;
She never chose unrighteous sons to rear.
She will not speak thy praises, if she hear
Thy wrong to me, thy wrong to God on high,
Wrought on His suppliants in their misery.
Would I, suppose my foot were on thy soil,
Without due permit from its King, take spoil
And ransom? Nay, although as clear as day
My rights were, I should know too well what way
Of life is seemly in an alien land.
But thou on thine own Thebes hast laid a brand
Of shame that she deserves not. Age hath brought
Grey hairs to thee, but no grey powers of thought.
Therefore I tell thee again, and thou take heed:
Have those two maids brought hither with all speed
Unless thou wouldst make longer in the land
Thy much enforcèd sojourn. This command
Comes not from my lips only but my heart.

LEADER

Stranger, 'tis so. Of righteous blood thou art
And noble, but thy deeds belie thy blood.

CREON

Neither in counsel nor in hardihood
Lacking, O Son of Aigeus, did I deem
Thy folk; but entering here, how could I dream
So strong a fancy for my kinsfolk would
Possess them, as to claim them theirs for good,
Against my will? I felt full sure beside
Athens would scarce receive a parricide,
A man incestuous, known to all as one
Stained by a mother coupling with her son:
Full sure the wisdom that in Ares' Rock
Is rooted ne'er would take wayfaring folk
Of that sort in her sacred boundaries.
In such belief I sought to take my prize.
Nor, even so thinking, had I turned to force,
Until on me and mine he laid a curse
Most deadly. Whereupon, being wronged, to smite
The wrongdoer I reckoned but my right.
For anger ages not, but burns till death.
Only dead men no dolour wakeneth.
Take, therefore, whatso action pleaseth thee,
Since I, though just my cause, am solitary
And powerless; yet for all my weakness I
Some day will to thy deeds with deeds reply.

OEDIPUS

O shameless heart! And think'st thou to have thrown
On my grey head these horrors or thine own?
Hast cried aloud that stain of kindred gore,
Incest and desolation, which I bore
But willed not? 'Twas, methinks, the wrath divine
Against some dark forefather of my line,
Not me; in me what evil can ye find
For which I should be cursed with crimes so blind
'Gainst mine, and me? The oracle had said
My father . . . 'twas God's doom . . . should be struck
      dead
By his own son. Am I to be believed
Guilty, I, unbegotten, unconceived,
Unborn? And if thereafter, born to doom
Like that, I met and slew, not knowing whom
I slew nor what I did, my father, who
Can charge on me the crime I never knew
Nor willed? And then my mother, she, thine own
Sister, whose shame with gibes thou harpest on,
And seek'st to make me speak . . . Aye, speak I will,
Since thou of foulest talk hast had thy fill.
She was, she was, my mother . . . Misery! . . .
My mother, when I knew it not, nor she,
And to her shame bore children to the son
Herself had borne. But thou, what hast thou done?
With full will thou hast wakened, with full will,
My shame and hers. I did my deed of ill
Unwilling, and unwilling I speak now.
And this I say, that vainly seekest thou,

Or in that deed or in my father's death,
Which everlastingly with bitter breath
Thou hurl'st against me, a fair ground to call
Me evil. This thing answer me withal.
If, here and now, some stranger came and sought
To kill thee, thee, so strict in deed and thought,
Wouldst question: "Is this unknown man by chance
My father?" or strike quickly in defence.
Smite him, I think, if still thou lov'st the light,
Not look around thee for thy legal right.
In such a pass, by God bewildered, then
I strove. Oh, were my father risen again
I think, I think, himself would pardon me.
But thou . . . not righteous art thou, only free
To fling foul condemnations, mouth at will
Things speakable and things unspeakable,
All to defile me here before the eyes
Of strangers. Aye, and thou hast found it wise
To praise the fame of Theseus and of great
Athens, the just, the law-abiding state;
But this forgettest, that, if any land
On earth hath piety to understand
The gods' due rites, 'tis Athens; and 'tis there
Thou darest from the hearth of God to tear
This age-worn suppliant, violent hands to lay
On me, and my two daughters bear away.
Wherefore in prayer I lift my voice to these
Dread Goddesses against such enemies
To give due aid, so thou shalt learn ere long
What breed of men defends this land from wrong.

81   F

LEADER

This man, though dogged by dire calamity,
Is noble, Sire, and meet for help from thee.

THESEUS

Enough! Or shall the plunderers of the land
Escape while we, their victims, idly stand?

CREON

Speak thy commands to one whose light is low.

THESEUS

Thou lead me on their track. Myself will go
To escort thee. If thou hast hid the maids hard by,
Reveal them to me. If their slavers fly
Far off we need not trouble. There be those
Gone forth whose nets even now about them close;
They will not thank their gods for passage fair!
Lead on; but know the hand that set the snare
Is now ensnared. The hunter is the prey.
The prizes of such treason melt away
Full fast. Nor think of helpers; though I guess
That never to such pride of recklessness
Hadst thou advanced unarmed or unallied.
Was there help here in which thou durst confide?
That I must watch. My city neither can,
Nor shall, be weaker than one lawless man.
Dost understand at all? Or is it in vain
I spoke to thee before, and speak again?

CREON

I came not here thy charges to deny;
At home I shall know well how to reply.

THESEUS

Threaten thy fill but go. Thou, Oedipus,
Remain in peace, putting full trust in us.
I swear, unless I die, I will restore
Right soon the daughters whom thou longest for.

OEDIPUS

Theseus, may God reward thy nobleness,
And this foresheltering aid for my distress.
                    [*Exeunt* THESEUS *and* CREON.

CHORUS

It is there that I would be,
          Where the foemen turn at bay,
With a shout, no more to flee,
          But confront us in the fray;
Be it inland where the Great Rocks soar,
Or amid the lit torches of the shore,
Where an old rite is cherished and made young
          By the Holy Ones whose high golden Key
Of Silence is laid upon the tongue
          Of the grave Eumolpidae.
Is it there our Prince's word
          With a war-cry strong to save

Shall awake the sleeping sword
  Ere the border line be passed,
And beside those sisters brave
   Stand at last?

Or it may be, drawing nigh
  By the northward and the west
To the pastures lying high
  Beneath Oïê's snowy crest,
They are rushing in a rivalry of speed
On chariots or on steed outvying steed.
Oh, ours shall be the prize! Dread in fight
Are the lances of Colonus; very dread
Is the cavalry of Theseus, borne ahead
  With bridles flashing bright.
 For Athena they will ride,
 In their harness full of pride;
 For above them watcheth She
  With the Shaker of the Earth,
 Whom the Horse loves and the Sea,
   Rhea's birth.

They strike; or do they wait their hour?
  A hope is whispering in my brain,
Of sudden weakening in the power
  Of evil o'er those captives twain
Much-suffering, who have found in these
Their kinsmen their worst enemies.
Ere evening falleth Zeus shall send
Fulfilment of a wondrous end;

The voices of my heart foretell
A day of battle ended well.
But, Oh, amid the clouds to fly
    On storm-swift pinions of a dove,
And, sudden, with far-ranging eye,
    Sweep on the battle from above!

O Thou above all gods that are,
    All-seeing eye, all-ruling hand,
Great Zeus, we pray thee, in this war
    Give strength to them who rule our land;
And with thee let Athena be,
Thy daughter, robed in majesty.
And, oh, ye twain in swift array,
Apollo, Hunter of the Prey,
And Artemis, the Archer Maid,
    Fleet follower of the dappled doe
Fast-flying, come, a twofold aid;
    To us and ours your mercy show!

Enter THESEUS *with Guards escorting* ANTIGONE
    and ISMENE.

LEADER

Ah, wanderer, mark! Not false the prophecy
Of us, thy watchers. Yonder I descry
The maidens with their escort drawing near.

OEDIPUS

Where? Where? What sayst thou?

ANTIGONE

                Father! Father dear!
Would that some god could give thee power to see
This brave man who has brought us back to thee!

OEDIPUS

Child, are ye both here?

ANTIGONE

            Yes. 'Tis Theseus' arm,
With his true guards, hath saved us from all harm.

OEDIPUS

Come to me, child, and let me feel once more
Those dear arms that so long I looked not for!

ANTIGONE

Thy prayer is mine. 'Tis what I long for most.

OEDIPUS

Where are ye? Where?

ANTIGONE

          Here, both. We are not lost.

OEDIPUS

Sweet flowers!

ANTIGONE

All fathers of their own are fain.

OEDIPUS

Props of my age!

ANTIGONE

And partners of thy pain.
[*The two daughters embrace their father.*

OEDIPUS

I hold my best beloved, and cannot be
Living or dead, unhappy utterly,
With you beside me. Press my body, so,
Children, on either side. Come closer. Grow
Into your father's being. Breathe again
From that hard path of loneliness and pain.
And quickly as ye may . . . brief speech is well
For maidens such as you . . . say what befell.

ANTIGONE

Here stands our champion. As the deed was his,
His be the tale. My task the lighter is.

OEDIPUS   [*To* THESEUS.

Thy pardon, if too long, too eagerly,
I have greeted these, mine own, restored to me
Past hope. I know through thee, through thee alone,
Like light upon our eyes, this joy hath shone.

87

'Tis thou, hast saved them. May the all-powerful God
Grant such reward as I, the powerless, would,
To thee and to this land. For here I find
Alone among the cities of mankind
Honour and godliness and truth. Even so
I speak her praise, and what I speak I know,
Seeing all I have, O King, I have through thee.
Reach out, I pray thee, thy right hand for me
To clasp it close, friend, aye, and if I may,
To kiss thy cheek . . . Alas, what would I say?
Wretch that I am, how could I ask that thou
Shouldst bear the touch of one upon whose brow
Is burned every pollution that man knows . . .
I ask not, nor will suffer it. 'Tis those
Only who have my burden borne, may share
With me my desolation. Nay, stand there
Apart; I still can bless thee, friend, and thou
Still grant me the same righteous care as now.

THESEUS

I marvel not that, having thus re-won
Thy lost ones, long in joy thy speech hath run,
Nor yet that their sweet greeting before mine
Hath claimed thy welcome. Why should I repine?
'Tis by deeds done I fain would seek to gird
My life to greatness, not the spoken word.
See, Father, have I failed in aught I swore
To do? Have I not brought them here, before
Thine eyes, alive, by all those menaces
Unscarred? About the fray scarce mine it is

To speak. Thou hast those with thee who, I know
Will tell thee all. But, prithee, here bestow
Thy thought. There came a tale to me but now,
As here I came; no great thing, yet, I vow,
Strange; and the smallest thing may call for thought.

OEDIPUS

What is it, Son of Aigeus? I know naught
Of what thou hast heard; say how the story ran.

THESEUS

Some man, thy kin but not thy countryman,
Hath cast him suppliant, I know not how,
On the Altar of Poseidon, where but now
I stood at sacrifice ere here I came.

OEDIPUS

Whence comes he? What doth his petition claim?

THESEUS

I know but one thing; speech with thee, they say,
He seeks, not long, not grievous any way.

OEDIPUS

To what end? Thus to kneel hath import grave.

THESEUS

Some speech with thee; that only doth he crave,
And then a safe return by the same road.

OEDIPUS

Who can it be who thus implores the God?

THESEUS

Think if in Argos any of thy race
Hath settled, who might seek to win thy grace.

OEDIPUS   [*Trembling.*

O friend! Peace! No word more!

THESEUS

        What shakes thee so?

OEDIPUS

Ask me not that!

THESEUS

        What? Tell me all.

OEDIPUS

        I know
That suppliant. Thy last question tells me all.

THESEUS

On whom could it with such dire meaning fall?

OEDIPUS

My son, O King, the accursèd, whom to hear,
Were anguish, like none other, to mine ear.

Theseus

Canst thou not hear him without doing aught
Thou wouldst not? The mere hearing hurts thee not.

Oedipus

That voice, my son's, rings hateful to his sire.
Compel me not to yield him his desire.

Theseus

The suppliant's knee is a compulsion hard
To escape. The God too claimeth due regard.

Antigone

O Father, hear my word, though I be still
But young in counsel. Let Theseus fulfill
His own heart's prompting and the God revere.
For our sake, too, admit our brother here
To implore thee. He cannot force thee to revoke
Thy purpose—fear it not—by mere words spoke
Unwisely. But to hear him. . . . where can be
The harm in that? And if some treachery
Be brewing, speech will bring it to the test.
He is thy child, and though the cruellest
Of wrongs and most ungodly he had wrought
On thee, thou, Father, must requite him not.
Oh, let him come! Men have had evil sons
Ere now, and hot wrath, yet the gentle tones
Of counsel and the prayers of friends have power
Softly to charm away their evil hour.

Ah, turn again, remember what dire woe
From sire, from mother, smote thee long ago.
Look to those days; and think on what a path
Thou then wast guided by this fire of wrath.
Alas, a living monitor thou hast
In those dark orbs, that light for ever lost.
Oh, yield to us! Dost see not? It is wrong
That those who pray for justice should pray long;
Or one who hath received great love should yet
Make no requital but stand obdurate.

OEDIPUS

Daughter, a grievous grace ye win from me,
Pleading; but as ye will so let it be.
Yet, if that man must come to me and speak . . .
This only, Friend, I ask, that none shall seek
Again to hold my body in his sway.

THESEUS

Enough. That word once spoken I obey,
Old Prince. No boast I speak but promise true,
The god that guardeth me shall guard thee too.

[*Exit* THESEUS.

CHORUS

Who craveth more and ever more
    Of life, beyond his lotted span,
As one astray and cleaving sore
    To the wrong road I judge that man.

The stores his long days may have won
    Move nearer suffering and defeat;
And joy—he knows not where 'tis gone,
    When life lags longer than is meet,
Till one Deliverer from all wrong
    The unseen portal openeth,
Where lives no love, no lyre, no song,
    Only the last thing, Death.

Not to be born, by all acclaim,
    Were best; but once that gate be passed,
To hasten thither whence he came
    Is man's next prize—and fast, Oh fast!
For, once he has unloosed his hand
    From Youth and Youth's light vanities,
What blow can from his path be banned?
    What griefs will not be surely his?
Strife, envy, falseness, blood and hate,
    Till, last, the curse of curses, lone,
Despised, weak, friendless, desolate,
    Old age hath claimed his own.

We are old and know suffering; but dread
    Is the doom of this stranger at the door.
Like a wave-lashed and winter-beaten shore,
    By the tempests of the North overrun,
The cold storms beat upon his head:
There is storm from the sinking of the sun,
    And storm from his first going forth,
Storm from the noon-tide's light,
Storm from the mountains of the night,
    And the wild winds of the north.

ANTIGONE

Ah, yonder! 'Tis that suppliant, meseems,
Alone, untended. Father, his cheek streams
With tears new-shed. 'Tis thee he seeks to find.

OEDIPUS

Who is he?

ANTIGONE

Who but he that in our mind
Hath been so long. Tis Polynîcês here.
    [*Enter* POLYNICES; OEDIPUS *turns away.*

POLYNICES

What shall I do? God help me, should this tear,
Sisters, be shed for sufferings of my own
Or his, my father's, aged and alone
Save for you two, in a strange land outcast,
In such a garb! Its ancient filth has passed
Into his withered flesh, infecting all
His flank; and o'er that eyeless face withal
Long hair untended tosses in the wind.
And food; poor fragments of a beggar's kind
His nurture! Oh, I am accurst, accurst,
To have learnt all this too late! Let me be first
Now to bear witness that in villainy
Most vile am I, thus to have tended thee!
Hear what I am from no lips but my own.
Yet doth not Mercy share the supreme throne

94

Of Zeus in all his doings? Let her win
A place in thy heart, Father; for my sin
May yet be atoned, made worse it cannot be.
Why art thou silent?
O Father, speak! Turn not away from me!
Wilt answer nothing, but in silent scorn
Reject me? Can that wrath that long hath torn
Thy heart not speak? O ye, sprung from his seed,
My sisters, try to move in my dire need
Those lips implacable, inexorable!
A suppliant here I kneel. It is not well
To turn me thus, without a word, away.

[OEDIPUS *remains silent.*

ANTIGONE

Unhappy one, speak thou. Say all thy say.
A flow of words may waken some old joys,
Sorrows, or pities, that may render voice
Back to the lips that had no voice before.

POLYNICES

So be it. I will speak out. I thank thee for
That counsel. First, I summon to mine aid
The God himself, at whose feet I was laid
When the King raised me up and hither sent
To speak and hear, with due enfranchisement
Of safe return; which safety I require,
Strangers, from you, my sisters, and my sire.

Now, I will tell thee, Father, why I came.
I am an outcast from my home, in shame

And banishment, because, as elder son,
I claimed to sit upon thy sovereign throne;
Whence Eteoclês, my younger, by no right
Of law, by no ordeal of armèd might,
Cozening the people's favour, had me cast
To banishment. Whereof the first and last
Cause I pronounce the Curse that clings to thee,
No act of mine. And so our seers decree.
Straightway to Dorian Argos did I bring
My cause. I won the daughter of the King
Adrastus. Then by oaths to me I bound
Them that for deeds of war were most renowned
In Argos. With their aid I now advance
A sevenfold host, good wielders of the lance,
'Gainst Thebes, and either in just battle die
Or cast the usurper down . . . Wilt ask me why
I have now come hither? 'Tis a suppliant call
And prayer to thee, Father, from me and all
My host that round the plain of Thêbê stands,
Seven mighty spearmen, seven united bands.
Great Amphiaraüs, first in fight, is there,
And first in all the auguries of the air;
The Aetolian son of Oineus with his Vine,
Tydeus; Eteoclus, of true Argive line;
Hippomedon, sent by Talaos, his sire;
Great Capaneus, who swears to burn with fire
The tower of Thebes. Then from Arcadia came
A knight who bears his warrior-mother's name,
That Maid so long by lovers unbeguiled,
Parthenopaeus, Atalanta's child.

The chief am I, thy first-born—or if not
Thy son, then by some demon fate begot—
To lead 'gainst Thebes the dauntless Argive spear.
All these, by whatsoe'er to thee is dear,
Home, child, or life, implore thee to forget
Thy heavy wrath 'gainst me, who now am set
Forth to chastise that brother who hath banned
My right and robbed me of my fatherland.
The oracles—if aught of truth there be
In oracles—have spoke: whoso from thee
Hath blessing shall the key of victory hold.
Oh, by our springs and fountains, by the old
Gods of our race, be softened! Look on me;
Like thee I am a beggar, and like thee
In a strange land. Like thee I have no home,
Saving by court to strangers. The same doom
Imprisons both, while yonder in our house
The usurper in his pride makes mock of us.
Father, if thou wilt join thy heart to ours,
With little time or toil my gathered powers
Will break his fences, lead thee to thy throne,
'Stablish in right thy honour and my own,
And drive him to the winds. If thy good will
Is with me all this hope I can fulfil:
Without thee, I shall not return alive.

[OEDIPUS *stands silent.*

LEADER

Nay, for the sender's sake some answer give,
Or good or ill, e'er he be turned away.

OEDIPUS

Lords of Colônus, hearken what I say.

Were this not Theseus' charge; had he not stirred
My heart to grant this man an answering word,
He ne'er had heard my voice. But be it so!
He shall not hence without an answer go,
And such an answer as shall bring, I trow,
Joy to his life no more. . . . Thou traitor, thou!
Thou, when thou hadst the sceptre and the throne
Which now thy brother holdeth for his own,
Didst me, thy father, drive unfriended, out
To exile; thou didst cast these rags about
My beggared frame, which now, made one with me
In toil and suffering, thou weepst to see.
I shed no tears. I bear what I must bear
Till death, remembering thee, my murderer.
'Tis thou hast made me thus to live in woe;
Thou hast cast me out. 'Tis by thy deed I go
A wanderer, begging from strange hands my lot
Of daily bread; and, had I not begot
These daughters, my true help, in certainty
I had died long since, for any aid from thee.
These girls have fed me, these preserve me, these
Are men, not women, for hard services.
But ye two brothers, ye are bastard blood,
Not sons of mine. Therefore the eye of God
Is burning—but not yet with all the hate
Stored for thine armies by the Theban gate.
Thou shalt not take that city. Thou shalt die
Blood-stained in sin, and with thy brother lie.

So ran the curse that my soul sent before
Against you, and now calls to rise once more
To fight my battle, that ye two may deign
To reverence your begetters, and refrain
From trampling on an eyeless man, brought low
By sons like you. These two girls did not so.
Thy right of royal birth, thy suppliant's cry,
This curse annuls for ever, while on high
At the right hand of Zeus Justice shall hold
Her seat, true guardian of the laws of old.
Begone, thou thing abhorred and fatherless,
And with thee take, most foul in wickedness,
These words of doom, the last gift of my hand.
Thou shalt not wreck by war thy fatherland;
Thou shalt not back to Argos make thy way;
By hand of kindred thou shalt die, and slay
Dying, the man who flung thee from the throne.
Such doom I speak, and call in prayer the lone
Darkness from which we spring, that home again
It take thee, never more to dwell with men.
I call the awful spirits of this glade,
I call Ares the Slayer, who hath laid
In your two hearts the seed of that dire hate . . .
Hear and begone! To all in Thebes relate,
And thine own host, how Oedipus outshares,
With his last word, his kingdom to his heirs.

LEADER

That e'er thou camest here, unhappy one,
My heart can feel no joy; and now, begone.

99

POLYNICES

Woe for my coming and my baffled quest!
Woe for my comrades! What an end unblest
To that proud march from Argos! Such an end—
I cannot speak thereof to any friend;
I cannot turn my army back. Woe's me!
Silent I go to meet my destiny.
O Sisters, ye his children, who have heard
Here at my side our father's ruthless word,
I charge ye, by God's mercy, when on me
That curse shall be fulfilled, if then you be
In Thebes and home, leave not my body all
Dishonoured; give me rites of burial
And unction. So the praises that ye two
Have earned from this man for your service true
Shall be again by other praise not less
Increased, for that last deed of faithfulness.

ANTIGONE

Brother! I pray, in one thing list to me!

POLYNICES

What wouldst thou? Speak, most dear Antigone.

ANTIGONE

Turn back thy host to Argos; quickly, now;
E'er all be lost, Thebes and thy friends and thou.

POLYNICES

It may not be. If I turn back, the men
I lead now ne'er would follow me again.

ANTIGONE

Again? But why again? What good should come
To thee, brother, from having wrecked thy home?

POLYNICES

'Tis base to stay an outcast, while his scorn
Mocks at my weakness, me his elder-born.

ANTIGONE

Dost seek to give thy father's prophecy
Fulfilment, dooming both to slay and die?

POLYNICES

'Tis what he wishes!—No. I cannot yield.

ANTIGONE

Woe's me! But who will follow to the field
Of battle when they hear those oracles?

POLYNICES

They will not hear them. A good leader tells
The heartening news. The worse must silent fall.

ANTIGONE

Brother! Thy will is fixed beyond recall?

POLYNICES

It is. Detain me not. A path is mine
To tread henceforth facing that doom, that sign
Of evil, planted by my sire and his
Avengers. Sisters, for you twain it is
My prayer that God may bless the paths ye tread;
Grant me but that one grace when I am dead;
I shall not ask another. Let me go,
And fare ye well, both.

ANTIGONE

Woe for ever, woe!

POLYNICES

Weep not for me.

ANTIGONE

Who could her weeping hide
When to stark death thou marchest open-eyed?

POLYNICES

I die when I needs must.

ANTIGONE

Friend! For my sake . . .

POLYNICES

No more vain pleading!

ANTIGONE

     Oh, my heart will break

If I lose thee!

POLYNICES

   Thus or some other way;
Fate will decide. But for you twain I pray
That God protect you from all ill; for ye
By all your deeds deserve not misery.

   [*Exit* POLYNICES. *Low thunder is heard far off.*

CHORUS

New threatenings of wrath before us loom
  From this man old and blind;
  'Tis evil, fraught with doom;
Or doth perchance some heavenly purpose find
  Its end here, some decree
Of God that without aim can never be?
For Time's eye watcheth, watcheth, to undo
The strong, and on the morrow to make new.

       Loud Thunder.

  O voice of Heaven! O Zeus!

OEDIPUS

O children, children! Haste. Whom can ye send
For Theseus, in this need my truest friend?

ANTIGONE

Father, what is there thou wouldst have him do?

OEDIPUS

This winged thunder of Zeus will guide my way
Even now to Hades. Send. Make no delay.

Thunder as before.

CHORUS

Ah 'tis the hand of God! It crashes there
    Again, unspeakable.
    My head is stabbed with fear,
And all my spirit cowers beneath its spell,
    Striking from sky to earth.
What new thing from these signs shall come to birth?
I tremble. Meaningless it cannot be.
Such wrath, nor fall without calamity.
    O voice of Heaven! O Zeus!

OEDIPUS

Daughters, the fated end of life is come
Upon me. I cannot fly nor turn therefrom.

ANTIGONE

Thou know'st? Some sign is here that tells thee true?

OEDIPUS

Most sure I know it. Send some messenger
With speed to lead the Lord of Athens here.

More Thunder.

Chorus

Ah, list! Once again, piercing, echoing round . . .
    Be merciful, O our God, merciful! . . . peals that
    sound.
Though upon Earth the All-Mother thine anger fall,
    Mercy, O God, for me! Let me not, if mine eye
    Has looked on a man of sin, share in his sin and die!

Oedipus

Is Theseus near, my daughter? Will he find
Me still in life and master of my mind?

Antigone

What prayer hast thou to press,
What pledge of faithfulness?

Oedipus

He helped my need. I would fulfil this day
The pledge I gave, and his good gift repay.

Chorus

Hither, my prince, oh, swift! Up from the inmost shade
    Of that sea-altar rise. Thy sacrifice is paid.
    'Tis thee that his needs invoke,
    Thy city and all thy folk.
He craveth the price to pay for thy love, thy harbouring.
    Hither! Be swift, O King.

                    [*Enter* Theseus.

THESEUS

Why this new clamour rising from you all?
I hear my people's voice, I hear the call
Of this my guest. Say not some thunderstroke
Or storm of lashing hail from Zeus hath broke
Upon you—though no terror were amiss
When heaven is opened in such rage as this.

OEDIPUS

O King, I pined for thee. 'Tis thou indeed?
Praise God thou art with me in my hour of need!

THESEUS

What new need is upon thee, Laïus' son?

OEDIPUS

My life's last hour. I would not leave undone
What I have vowed to Athens, when I die.

THESEUS

What signs are here of such calamity?

OEDIPUS

The gods are their own heralds. They have told
Their tale, naught failing from their words of old.

THESEUS

Old sufferer, how do they their doom reveal?

OEDIPUS

This never-ceasing thunder, peal on peal,
Doth speak their message, and yon levin brand
That lightens in the unconquerable hand.   [*Thunder*

THESEUS

Thou conquerest me. These signs have proved thee true
And filled with power. Tell me what thing to do.

OEDIPUS

Theseus, for thee and thine I will unfold
A secret that shall live and grow not old.
Myself first, with no aid of hand or eye,
Will lead thee to the place where I must die.
Which place reveal thou never, nor the guise
It beareth, nor the region where it lies;
So shalt thou gain a stronger fence from harm
Than many a shield or many an allied arm. . . .
More things there be to tell thee, but no speech
May wake them yet; when thou and I shall reach
That place alone, with no man near us, then
'Tis thine to know them. For no sons of men,
Not these, not mine own children, whom I love,
Shall ever from my lips hear word thereof.
Guard them thyself alone. And when thy share
Of life draws near its end, then to thine heir
Reveal the tale, and he to his; and so
For ever more. Thus shall thy city go
Her ways unravaged by the Dragon's Brood.
Else . . . crowding round thee, though thy deeds be good,
Are cities that will lightly turn to wrong.
For God is slow to smite: yet sure and strong
His judgement upon them that go astray
From godliness and turn the madman's way.

O Son of Aigeus, seek not thou to go
That road . . . But all this it was thine to know
Long since. And that which from the God is come
Doth urge me. Let us on to my dark home
Nor scruple more. Ye Daughters, to my side
Come, both. Henceforth I am become your guide,
Whom once ye guided. Come, but touch me not.
Myself alone will find that holy spot
Where hid for ever I shall lie. This way;
So; come this way. Soul-guiding Hermes goes
Before and She whose name the Darkness knows . . .
O Lamp unlit, the only light of old
To these wrecked eyes, for the last time thy hold
Is on me. Yea, it looseth as I go
To hide my blindness and my wrongs below
Where Hades dwells . . . O friend, O helping hand,
Blessed be thou, thy lieges and thy land,
Remembering one here hidden, one who trod
Through sin, through death, the path ordained of God.

[*Exeunt* OEDIPUS, THESEUS *and the* SISTERS.

CHORUS

To the Bride whom none beholdeth,
And to thee, Lord of the Dying,
To the calm seats that enthrone you,
To the dark where none hath known you,
We uplift our adoration;
Lo, I name thee, kneeling, crying,
Aïdôneu, Aïdôneu!

Not in torment, we beseech thee,
Not with noise of lamentation,
May he strive to thee and reach thee,
Through the fields that fear enfoldeth,
Through the shadow-haunted City.
He hath borne enough of sorrow;
God is just and shall have pity,
Shall have mercy on the morrow.
Aïdôneu, Aïdôneu !

There be noises of disaster,
There be goddess-shapes infernal,
And beyond the crowded portal—
So men whisper and refrain not—
Lo, a wild beast body lying
And the voice of one that ravens,
One that sleeps not, one immortal,
Watching, gnarling, from his caverns.

Still them, Thou that art their master,
Thou, O Terrene, O Nocturnal!
Let them slumber and complain not;
Let them cease and leave this mortal
Passage, where the gates are parted,
Through the turmoil of the dying,
Through the dreams of the departed,
Home to Thee, O Sleep Eternal!

[*Enter a* MESSENGER.

MESSENGER

Athenians, in the briefest shape I may
I tell you: Oedipus hath passed away.
But all his doings cannot in a few
Light words be told. Not light they were to do.

LEADER

How? Is he dead?

MESSENGER

Most surely from the sight
Of man he hath passed, and left the realms of light.

LEADER

Some griefless stroke from heaven upon him fell?

MESSENGER

Thou hast said it. 'Tis a wondrous tale to tell.
How from this place he started, thou wilt know,
Who saw him, with no guide, no friend to show
The way, himself a leader to us all.
So came he to that threshold mystical
Of Earth, deep-rooted by the Brazen Stair
Precipitous. Many branching paths are there.
He made his choice among them, till he stayed
Close by the basoned rock where Theseus laid
The inviolate memorial of his pledge
Sworn to Pirithoüs, near the bason's edge,

Midway between that Stone of Triple Plume,
The hollow Pear-tree and the marble tomb.
There pausing he sat down and loosed withal
His sordid raiment. Then with a proud call
He charged his daughters water from the spring
To find, for cleansing and for offering
Libation. Swift to do their father's will,
The maidens sped to where Dêmêtêr's Hill,
Green with the goddess' gift, stood clear to view.
They brought the water, and with ritual due
Prepared him, and the raiment of the grave
About him wrapped; then, when his heart could crave
No more of service, and there rested naught
Undone of the lustration that he sought,
God's voice beneath us thundered. At that sound
The maidens sank to earth in tears, and wound
Their arms about his knee and beat their breast.
He heard their sudden cry of grief, and pressed
Both to his arms: "My children, from this day
You have no father. All is passed away
That once was mine or me, and all the sore
Toils of my tendance shall be yours no more;
Hard toils, I know well; yet one word there is
That maketh light your heaviest services.
Love I have given you, such as none beside
Could give. But now alone ye shall abide
And orphaned of that love through all your days."

    So, clinging close and sobbing in amaze,
All wept; but when the rite of tears was o'er,
And that lamenting cry arose no more,

Deep silence fell; then on the silence brake
A great voice calling. All our hearts did shake
With fear and our hair stiffened, for all round
Like many divine voices, rose that sound:
"Ho Thou! Thou Oedipus! Why do we stay
Our goings? All too long is thy delay."
He heard, and, hearing, knew God's summons clear.
Straightway he called that Theseus be brought near,
And when he came, "O friend," he cried," in troth
Give me thy right hand—man's most ancient oath—
Clasp it, my daughters!—never to forsake
These twain but act in all things for their sake
As love will prompt." And he, as a true friend,
Unshrinking, vowed in good faith to the end
To observe his promise. Once that deed was done,
The father laid his groping hands upon
His children's heads and spake: "Be strong of heart,
Daughters! From this place ye must now depart.
Seek not to see forbidden sights, or hear
Words spoken that are not for mortal ear.
Go with all haste. Theseus, alone with me,
Hath right this secret thing to hear and see."

We all had heard his charge, and, with lament
And tears, followed the maidens as they went.
At last, we turned again to look; and there,
Long gazing, him we saw not anywhere,
But Theseus standing all alone, his hand
Across his face uplifted, to withstand
The sight of some dread vision which no eye
Of mortal might endure. To Earth and Sky,

To Mother Earth and Sky the House of God,
We saw him, in one movement where he stood,
Make prayer.
    And what way Oedipus hath gone
From life none knoweth save Theseus alone.
For sure there came no visible death, no sweep
Of fire from God, no storm-wind of the deep;
But or some guide was sent from heaven above,
Or yawned the firmament of death, in love
And mercy, to receive him without pain.
For not in mortal anguish was he ta'en,
Nor sickness nor lament, but in a dream
Of wonder. For this tale if any deem
Me mad . . . for such, I care not what they say.
       [*Exit* MESSENGER.

LEADER

The daughters and their escort, where are they?
Not far, methinks. Those voices that we hear
Lamenting show the maidens drawing near.
      [*Enter* ANTIGONE *and* ISMENE.

ANTIGONE

Misery, misery! What can remain for us, twain in
   unhappiness, utterly naught?
Only to look on this curse that hath lain on us, born of
   our father's blood, never forgot;
Long as he lived we have served him unrestingly.
Now, at the last, what saw we, what suffered we?
   An end too strange for thought.

LEADER

What is that end?

ANTIGONE

We know not, only guess.

LEADER

Gone is he?

ANTIGONE

Gone, methinks, in blessedness.
How say ye? He to whom there came
No stroke of war nor stormy seas,
But unseen regions without name
Rapt him to their great silences.
For us, a darkness of the grave
Heavy upon our eyelid stays;
On what far land or tossing wave
Shall we two wander through our weary days?

ISMENE

I know not, sister, I, forlorn!
I would that Hades' hand of fire
Would give me rest beside my wearied sire;
For that which cometh is not to be borne.

LEADER

Bravest of daughters, sisters one in fame,
'Tis wisdom where life leadeth to be led.
Stir not your hearts to flame;
Not without glory is the path ye tread.

ANTIGONE

Even for sorrow the heart of mortality craveth in
     memory once it is past;
That which was sorely unsweet could be sweet to me,
     father and sorrow together held fast.
Father, belovèd one, thou that hast covered thee
Deep in the darkness, still reacheth our love to thee—
     Her love and mine shall last.

LEADER

His end was . . .

ANTIGONE

Even the end he hungered for.

LEADER

What wise?

ANTIGONE

Upon a strange yet chosen shore;
For ever in a shaded sleep
    Below the realm of light he lies,
While those he left are left to weep.
    Dost see, Father, my streaming eyes?
I know not how to crush, to lay
    In nothingness, such grief as mine;
To die unknown, the wish was thine;
But must I give thee nothing on thy way?

ISMENE

Alas, what fate abideth thee and me,
Sister? For ever fatherless are we.

LEADER

Nay, sisters well-belovèd, since his life
   In happy wise is now unyoked and free,
     Cease from this mourning strife.
   Unsnared by sorrow can no mortal be.

ANTIGONE

Now haste we back!

ISMENE

What haste have we?

ANTIGONE

Desire constrains me.

ISMENE

What desire?

ANTIGONE

That dark and earthly home to see.

ISMENE

Of whom?

ANTIGONE

Unhappy! Of our sire.

ISMENE

Can that be lawful? Seest thou not . . .?

ANTIGONE

What should I see?

ISMENE

This too recall . . .

ANTIGONE

Thou chidest me?

ISMENE

He passed without
Or grave or rite, unseen of all.

ANTIGONE

Oh, take me where he died, and there
Slay me!

ISMENE

Alas, with neither friend
Nor hope, in what land shall I bear
My life to its last end?

LEADER

Ah, fear not!

ANTIGONE

Whither shall I fly?

LEADER

Your flights are ended.

ANTIGONE

In what home?

LEADER

Here, where all grief shall pass you by.

ANTIGONE

Nay; I have thoughts . . .

LEADER

Say where they roam.

ANTIGONE

Toward Thebes, our home; but how to go
I know not.

LEADER

That road seek not thou!
'Tis troublous, all.

ANTIGONE

'Twas alway so.

LEADER

Hopeless of old, more hopeless now.

A sea of storms is tossing there.

ANTIGONE

O Zeus, yet guide me to begone!
To what last hope, amid despair,
    Doth some god urge me on?   [*Enter* THESEUS.

THESEUS

Weep not, my children. Who would weep
    When Unseen Powers to quick and dead
    Alike a gracious end have sped.
Stir not the anger of the deep.

ANTIGONE

O Son of Aigeus, grant one thing . . .

THESEUS

My daughter, speak that one desire.

ANTIGONE

To see the tomb that holds our sire.

THESEUS

It may not be.

ANTIGONE

How so, O King?

THESEUS

Your sire on me this charge has thrown;
    No mortal shall approach that place,
    Nor lift a voice that tomb to grace
Wherein he sleeps, unseen, unknown.

Thus shall he keep my soil untrod
    By foeman's feet; his charge was clear;
    'Twas heard in Heaven: it reached the ear
Of Faith, the all-seeing Child of God.

ANTIGONE

If so our father wills, 'tis good.
    To ancient Thebes, then, let us speed;
    We still may stem, in hour of need,
The torrent of our brethren's blood.

THESEUS

That will I; and if aught avail
    To aid or you or him, yet new
    In his dark travel, him and you
I never shall betray nor fail.

CHORUS

Let there be Peace, O ye that mourn! Give o'er
Your vain lament; whate'er hath been before,
This that is done shall stand for ever more.

OEDIPUS:

THE PREVIOUS STORY

Laïus, king of Thebes, had kidnapped the beautiful son of his benefactor, Pelops. For this Apollo decreed that he must have no son himself; if he had, it would kill him and commit incest upon its mother, Jocasta. A son was born, and his parents exposed it to die on Mt. Kithairon, but a Corinthian shepherd found it and took it to Corinth, where it was named Oedipus and was reared as the son of the childless queen Merope and her husband Polybus. Hearing a taunt that he was no true son of Polybus, Oedipus inquired at Delphi, and the oracle, not answering his question, told him he was doomed to kill his father and wed his mother. Thinking this referred to Polybus and Merope, Oedipus fled away from Corinth. On his travel he was rudely struck and driven off the road by a stranger and in the ensuing fight killed him. The stranger was really Laïus. Coming to Thebes Oedipus found the city in distress, ravaged by the riddling Sphinx. The king was lost, and Creon, as governor, offered the crown and the hand of Jocasta to any one who would deliver the city. Oedipus faced the Sphinx, guessed her riddle, and accepted the prize. Later the city was visited by a plague; the Delphic oracle said this was because the murderer of Laïus was in the city, unknown. Oedipus vows to find him, and in an unshrinking search, even when he sees where it is leading, proves that the murderer is he himself. Jocasta kills herself; Oedipus puts out his eyes, so that he may never in the next life see his parents' faces. He begs to be cast out on the mountain to die as his parents had wished, but Creon refuses to do this till advice shall come from the oracle at Delphi. Later, apparently, he was cast out and would have died, had he not been tended by his daughter Antigone. His kingdom was divided between his sons, Eteocles and Polynices.

P. 17, l. 16, Ground profane or.] A holy place would be more undisturbed than the open road but not necessarily forbidden ground. The grove of the Eumenides was specially sacred and "untrodden."

P. 20, l. 42, Spirits of Mercy.] The Erinyes, or Furies, originally perhaps the spirits of the wronged dead calling for vengeance, were so formidable that they were generally known by some euphemistic name, *Semnai*, "The Venerable" or *Eumenides*, "Those of Good Will." But Oedipus has a special relation or kinship with them. Like them he is ancient and sad and craves for justice; and the oracle has foretold that in their shrine he shall find peace.

P. 21, l. 53 ff. On these local sanctities see Introduction p. 13.

P. 28, l. 174. He is leaving sanctuary and will be at their mercy.

P. 33, l. 245, Not blind.] That is, "You and I can look into each other's eyes and thus meet in human sympathy."

P. 34, l. 274, They planned my death.] The exposure of unwanted infants has been, throughout history, a common practice in times of distress. It is a frequent *ficelle* in Menander's plays. Here however it is treated as a cruel crime.

P. 36 f. The Ismene scene. See Introduction, p. 6.

P. 39, l. 337. In Egypt . . . men sitting at the loom. This is one of three passages in which Sophocles seems clearly to be borrowing from the book, or the public readings, of his friend Herodotus. See Hdt., ii, 35. The others are *Electra* 62, compared with the return of Zalmoxis in Hdt., iv, 95, and *Antigone*, 905 ff., on the irreplaceableness of a brother, compared with Hdt., iii, 119.

P. 39, l. 354, All oracles.] Notice how much the helpless and wronged old man, having no prospect of ordinary human aid, pins his hopes upon signs and oracles.

P. 40, l. 375, Polynices is here the elder; Eteoclês gets rid of him, not by any honourable means, such as ordeal by battle, but "by persuading the city." In Aeschylus' *Seven* and Euripides' *Phoenissae* Eteocles is the elder, but the two brothers, in order to avoid strife, have agreed to share the throne, reigning year and year about. Eteocles reigns first and refuses to resign at the end of the year.

P. 42, l. 406, Some Theban dust.] Even outside

Theban territory his body might have a casing of
Theban earth wrapped round it; in that case he would,
ritually, be buried in his native soil.

P. 44, ll. 431–444. This somewhat awkward and
elaborate argument is strictly in accord with the end
of *Oedipus Rex*. Perhaps the extraordinarily moving
prayer of Oedipus there, to be cast out to die on the
mountains, could not be forgotten either by Sophocles
or his audience. Otherwise it would have been much
simpler to avoid the story of the change of mind.
(Cf. 766 ff.)

P. 46, l. 470, With clean hands.] It is true that
Oedipus might make his hands ritually "clean" before
entering the precinct, but it looks as if he rather shrank
from the word and preferred that one of the daughters
should go.

P. 48, l. 486. The Merciful. See on l. 42.

Pp. 49–53, ll. 510–550. Chorus. One might have
thought that the horror expressed by the Elders at
their first hearing of the names of Laïus and Oedipus
was enough without this reinforcement of all the
details of Oedipus's incest and parricide. Evidently
Sophocles felt it necessary to emphasize strongly both
the "untouchableness" of Oedipus and the heroic
charity of Theseus. To an ancient audience Oedipus
bore a twofold stain of kindred blood, having com-
mitted the greatest offence possible against both father
and mother, and this produced a sentiment of religious
horror which we cannot quite feel.

P. 54, l. 562. This speech of Theseus is a typical

expression of Greek *Sophrosynê*, or "moderation," the opposite of *Hubris*.

P. 55, l. 576, My body . . . a gift.] See Introduction p. 10.

P. 58, l. 620, Thebes in armed array.] History, of course confirmed this prophecy. Thebes was a constant enemy of Athens.

Pp. 62–64, ll. 667–719. Chorus. This lyric, I think, is meant to suggest a fairly long space of time during which Oedipus has stayed in untroubled peace at Colonus, and further to show what a peaceful and heaven-protected place of rest he has at last found.

P. 62, l. 667. The Greek says merely "this well-horsed land"; but I think the meaning of the word is religious or mystical, like all the references in this ode. One of the great Attic legends tells of the contest between Athêna and Poseidon for the possession of Attica; as their rival gifts, Poseidon created the horse, Athêna the olive. The story typifies, no doubt, the contest between the *Pedieis*, or the people of the plain, and the *Paraloi*, those of the sea. (Cf. 59, 713, 1072.) The reference to the "young horses" as distinct from "the horses" is something to which we have no clue; the Olive is, of course, the sacred olive which the Persians burned but could not kill, when they destroyed the Acropolis in 480 B.C.

P. 63, l. 693, golden rein:] Aphrodite had a golden chariot.

P. 63, l. 704, orbed on high:] the orb of the sun was "Olive Zeus," the chief force that makes the olive grow.

P. 65, ll. 728 ff. Observe what a good case Creon makes for himself. Even his later speech in 939 ff., after he has put himself obviously in the wrong by his acts, is dignified and effective.

P. 66, l. 766, I prayed to be cast out.] Cf. on 431–444.

P. 67, l. 799, Cf. 870. Oedipus is in extreme misery; his curse on Creon emphasizes it; but at least he is not in the power of his enemies.

P. 73, l. 860. By ordinary Greek law Creon, as Antigone's uncle, is her natural guardian, her father being an exile without rights. But he has no right to kidnap her on Attic territory. Over Oedipus he has no rights, at any rate now that Oedipus is accepted as an Athenian citizen. (l. 637.)

P. 78, l. 919. This extremely respectful language towards Thebes herself is interesting. It suggests a political attitude: "The Thebans are quite good people, it is only the wicked anti-Athenian party in Thebes who make the trouble."

Pp. 83–85, ll. 1044–1095. Battles in Greek tragedy must always be "off stage" and are usually described in a Messenger's speech. The finest example is the description of the Battle of Salamis in the *Persae*. A lyric like this is hardly suitable for describing a battle, but can indicate the feelings and guesses of those who are left behind waiting for the result. For a much deeper and more tragic form of the same effect compare the prayers and terrified exclamations of the besieged women in Aeschylus' *Seven Against Thebes* (78–180).

P. 83, l. 1047. Be it inland etc. Cf. l. 900. The
Theban guards might have started by either of two
roads, one through the hills (by the pass of Daphne?),
one by the Bay of Eleusis, where torch-light processions
formed part of the Mysteries in worship of the Holy
goddesses, i.e. the Mother and the Maid, Demeter
and Korê. The Eumolpid family had certain hereditary
duties in Eleusinian worship, and the "key," or bar,
of silence was of course incumbent on all the initiated.

P. 84, l. 1072. Rhea's birth: Poseidon was the son
of Cronos and Rhea. Observe that in Sophocles there
is no conflict between Poseidon and Athena.

P. 88, l. 1131, Stand there apart:] The kiss of the
untouchable would be too much, even after his acceptance as a citizen. Theseus does stand far off.

P. 89, l. 1156, not thy countryman:] Polynices had
no doubt lost his Theban citizenship; at any rate he
had come from Argos.

P. 90, l. 1172, with such dire meaning fall:] That
is: "My last words, apparently harmless, seem to have
branded the man as evil or hostile."

P. 91, l. 1177. The actual sound of Polynices' voice
is pain to the blind man, as the voice of Creon was in
l. 863.

Pp. 92 f., ll. 1211–1249. Lyric on Old Age. Old age
was like Love and Death, a conventional subject for
gnomic poetry. In Stobaeus's *Anthology* three successive
chapters are "Praise of Age," "Dispraise of Age,"
"That Age can be borne well." The present ode
expresses well the feeling of the Elders when faced

with the misery and age of Oedipus, whose worst wish for Creon had been "an old age such as mine." (870) "Not to be born" is best for a man in the same sense in which "to have no history" is happiness for a nation; both are true if you count only "the crimes, follies, and disasters of mankind," leaving out the joys and achievements.

P. 95, l. 1281. An incomplete line, or rather two words spoken *extra metrum*.

P. 96, ll. 1284 ff. It was a proud achievement for a homeless exile, like Polynices, to inspire such confidence that Adrastus was willing to give him his daughter's hand and the seven great chiefs to make common cause with him. The list of the Seven is the same as in Aeschylus; in Euripides' *Phoenissae* the shadowy Eteoclus is omitted and Adrastus himself included.

P. 98, l. 1360. "I do not weep; I curse my enemy." I conquer sorrow and nurse undying anger.

P. 99, l. 1375, The curse . . . before:] After hearing Ismene's news (ll. 421 ff., 451 ff.)

P. 99, l. 1390. The lone Darkness from which we spring:] The conception seems to be that the accursed race has sprung from some special Erebos of its own, which can now receive Polynices to its home apart from all human kind.

P. 100, l. 1410. Polynices' prayer for due funeral rites turns one's mind at once to the *Antigone*. Cf. l. 1442. "If I lose thee," which shows the same special love for Polynices as in the *Antigone*.

P. 103, ll. 1447 ff., "Evil, fraught with doom."]
Oedipus is still a sinister figure, especially after his
curse upon his son. A little later on (l. 1483) he is still
"a man of sin" the mere sight of whom may be fatal.

P. 107, l. 1519. Having heard the divine summons
Oedipus is changed. It is like the change at l. 84 where,
as soon as the Stranger is gone, he turns in prayer to
the Eumenides: terrible to others, to him they are
kindred and friends. He has, of course, no thought of
forgiving his enemies or withdrawing his curse; his
curse is part of his supernatural power; but he has
turned to greater things.

P. 107, l. 1534, Dragon brood.] The teeth of the
Dragon that Cadmus killed were sown as seeds, and
from them sprang a harvest of armed men who fought
till only five were left. From those five the true Thebans
were descended.

P. 108, l. 1541, "That which from the god is come."]
It is not defined further. It is an inward feeling or
sense of command. Cf. the "guide" in l. 1661.

P. 108, l. 1549. The "Lamp unlit" is of course the
darkness that envelops the blind. Such darkness no
longer affects him.

P. 108 f., l. 1556 ff. This whole lyric has an echoing
liturgical effect. The mysterious name "Aïdôneus"
is a Homeric form of "Hades." In drama it occurs
only here and in the invocation of the ghost of Darius
in the *Persae*, ll. 649 ff. There too it is repeated twice.
The infernal goddesses would perhaps be such as
Persephone herself, Hecate, and certain avenging

spirits. The wailing recalls Cocytus, "the river of Wailing." The "wild beast body" and the ravening voice of course belong to the watch-dog of Hades, Cerberus.

P. 110 f., ll. 1587 ff. As the scholiast says, "These places are known to the natives."

The rock of triple plume.] There was such a rock at Colônus (Schol. on l. 57), so "three-crested" may well be the right word here in place of the MS "Thorycian rock." Thorycus was a deme in the extreme south of Attica, far away from Colônus. Observe that though these local details are given so exactly, evidently from local tradition, the site of the actual grave is known to none. Perhaps Sophocles is combining two different traditions by making the place where Oedipus was translated different from the place where his body was ultimately laid. Nothing is known of the pear tree or the marble tomb.

P. 110, l. 1594, Pledge.] It was in consequence of this pledge that Theseus, after vainly trying to dissuade Pirithoüs from his journey to Hades, was compelled to accompany him and to share his long imprisonment. The whole language here is more suited to the time of Sophocles than to the lifetime of Theseus himself.

P. 113, l. 1658, No visible death.] There had been storm and lightning just before, but at this moment there was nothing to account for the disappearance of Oedipus. It must have been some influence or "presence" from the Gods, or else perhaps the roof of Hades opened and the nether world received him.

P. 116, l. 1724, Can that be lawful?] Observe that Ismene is the wiser; Antigone is carried away by her feelings. Cf. l. 1756.

P. 120, l. 1769, Faith.] The Greek Horkos, "oath," is in its original meaning a "fence" or "sanction." When you have given your word there is some Thing or Spirit that binds you or "fences" you in; it is a "watcher of oaths." See *Rise of the Greek Epic*, Appendix D.

P., 120 l. 1770, Thebes.] They reach Thebes too late to stop the mutual slaying of the brothers; cf. the opening of the *Antigone*.

GEORGE ALLEN & UNWIN LTD
LONDON: 40 MUSEUM STREET, W.C.1
CAPE TOWN: 58–60 LONG STREET
SYDNEY, N.S.W.: 55 YORK STREET
TORONTO: 91 WELLINGTON STREET WEST
CALCUTTA: 17 CENTRAL AVE., P.O. DHARAMTALA
BOMBAY: 15 GRAHAM ROAD, BALLARD ESTATE
WELLINGTON, N.Z.: 8 KINGS CRESCENT, LOWER HUTT